Don't Mind Me, I Just Died

On Time, Tennis, and Unforgiving Mothers

Caroline Sutton

Don't Mind Me, I Just Died

On Time, Tennis,
and Unforgiving Mothers

Caroline Sutton

Montemayor Press
Montpelier, Vermont

For information contact:

Montemayor Press
P. O. Box 546, Montpelier, Vermont 05601
Web site: www.MontemayorPress.c om

1   3   5   7   9   10   8   6   4   2

Library of Congress Cataloging-in-Publication Data

  Names: Sutton, Caroline, 1953- author.
  Title: Don't mind me, I just died / Caroline Sutton.
  Description: First edition. | Montpelier, Vermont : Montemayor Press, 2017.

  Identifiers: LCCN 2016055610 (print) | LCCN 2017013335 (ebook) | ISBN
    9781932727210 (e-book) | ISBN 1932727213 (e-book) | ISBN 9781932727197
    (hardcover : alk. paper) | ISBN 1932727191 (hardcover : alk. paper) | ISBN
    9781932727203 (pbk. : alk. paper) | ISBN 1932727205 (pbk. : alk. paper)
  Subjects: LCSH: Sutton, Caroline, 1953---Family. | Authors, American--21st
    century--Family relationships. | Mothers and daughters. | Families | Life
    change events. | Death. | Authors, American--21st century--Biography.
  Classification: LCC PS3619.U893 (ebook) | LCC PS3619.U893 Z85 20017 (print) |
    DDC 814/.6 [B] --dc23
  LC record available at https://lccn.loc.gov/2016055610

Certain names of persons and places have been changed in the interests of privacy.

For my father, J. A. S.

We shall not cease from exploration
And the end of all our exploring
Will be to arrive where we started
And know the place for the first time.

—T. S Eliot, "Little Gidding"

Contents

Don't Mind Me, I Just Died

On Time, Tennis,
and Unforgiving Mothers

Author's Note

The essays that follow were written over a period of fourteen years during which my family, like any family, went through changes and rites of passage, kids growing up and leaving, parents aging. Central to the collection is my mother's decline and death. Since ends shed light on beginnings, and since memory itself is non-sequential, I've placed the story of her death, the title story, at the beginning. Other essays hop back in time to her life in a nursing home and before. Thematic threads rather than chronology connect the essays in each section, which exploits the possibilities of this genre of synthesis and seems fitting for the eclectic nature of experience and any attempt to reinvent it. C.S.

I want to thank the following literary magazines for their prior publication of my essays. "Questionable Paternity" appeared first in *North American Review.* "Slippery as a Salamander, Shifty as Light" and "Despite Her Pearls" were published first in *Tampa Review;* "Tennis: Fort-da!"* originally appeared in *The Literary Review;* "Water on Fire" in *Antigonish*; "To Arrest the Phases of the Moon" in *Cimarron Review;* "Don't Mind Me, I Just Died" in *Southwest Review,* and "How Could That Matter Now?" in *Fifth Wednesday.* An earlier version of "The Fly in the Refrigerator," previously titled "Getting Out of Newark," was published first in *Green Mountains Review.* "Missing" and "Fin" appeared first in *Ascent;* "Left Unhung" in *Your Impossible Voice;* "Circling the Pond" and an earlier version of "Recovering Time" were published originally in *The Rambler.* "Eclipsed" appeared first in *The Southern Humanities Review.* "With Her and Without" is reprinted by permission of *The Pinch,* copyright 2017 by Caroline Sutton.

I

Don't Mind Me, I Just Died

When I moved my mother from her independent apartment at the Quadrangle to assisted living, the supervisor handed me a clipboard with reams of papers to fill out. You might help her, they advised. Yes, given that my mother's obsessive efficiency had subsided, I would need to help. Otherwise the papers would languish under the Talbot's catalogs and AARP bills, many lines left out like missing teeth. I dashed off the perfunctory ones—birthday and marital status—but some were more personal. We want to get to know you. Favorite colors, favorite foods. Then it got deeper. Are you prone to depression? they asked. When you're feeling down, whom do you talk to? Chaddy (after her maiden name Chadwick-Collins) was glancing about her one room, which was smaller than the previous and lacking a fire-hazardous kitchenette. Her eyes were like chips of oak, her cheeks ruddy and rough like crushed brick. "Pokie, I guess."

After the insult, I began to wonder what she disclosed. When I was around she kept the banter with her Westie pretty mundane, the usual "good little Pokie," "go pee," "ata girl," "here's a nice biscuit," and so on. Here I thought I was the one. After a glass or two of wine, she would confide in me about my father's drinking, though he had died years before. At dinner parties, especially the ones related to the firm, she'd kick him under the table. Jim. Shouldn't we be getting home? In the inbred network of Philadelphia's Main Line in the '50s, she didn't dare tell even Boo or Mibbs, her best friends, though they'd gossip for hours downstairs while I tried to study. She was saving his career, she later said. She was also saving the family, and that was a matter of pride as well as money. And style. You just didn't go airing the family

1

laundry. We had a clothesline out back where the nanny hung our underwear, after all.

After the insult, I just felt sad.

Despite the kind intentions signaled by the questionnaire, no one in the Holly facility took much interest in my mother as far as I could tell. When I sat with her at lunch, she'd nod in the direction of an aide. Can't stand that one. Yanks the toothbrush right out of my hand. Admittedly, she might have kept brushing for a half hour. Still, there is dignity. As her lucidity gradually slipped away like saliva down a drain, I could no longer tell what was true. They tried to make her walk; they'd heave her up, grabbing under both arms. When they said lean forward, she'd lean back. They had me buy a springy pillow that sort of ejected her as they lifted. And she hated it all. She'd dig in and shake her head, not wanting to stand, this spirited woman who was born in 1918, went to Bryn Mawr College in the '30s, lived through World War II during which a man she scarcely knew asked her to marry him from an aircraft carrier in the South Pacific, came home, had a wedding on April Fool's, and left for a year. Who is this stranger, she thought on his return. It was kind of weird, she'd say. They stayed married until his death: 50 years, 8 months. No, she wouldn't get up for them. But if I told her we'd walk around the building with Pokie, sometimes she'd push forward and get her balance on her unblemished Reeboks, slowly moving her chunky legs in tan stretch pants from Lands End. (Oh, for willowy legs like Kate Hepburn's, we used to moan, turning before the mirror.) Now we trudged around, with Chaddy threatening to sit down on the occasional bench from which I'd never be able to get her up alone. After those visits I'd leave her in the dining room, all yellow Laura Ashley curtains and white tablecloths, with strangers who talked while she, the veteran talker, now just listened. Pokie would wait in her room, go out with the dog walker, and curl up on her red plaid bed. What would my mother tell her? That I hadn't stayed long enough? That we'd gone out for a nice piece of fish, though we hadn't? That the woman at her table was an insufferable bore? That she wondered if the primroses planted along the hedge by our old house had survived the unseasonable frost?

Then came an abuse case in Holly. So I figured Chaddy still knew a thing or two. As we received letters of assurance from the Quadrangle, my mother aspirated and nearly forgot how to swallow, so on she went to the final station, the one at the end of the line: skilled nursing. And Pokie went too.

This room was about the same size as the previous but lacked a rug and a chair. Around the hospital bed I arranged vestiges of the old house, her mahogany bureau with brass handles, her rose petal lamps, a big photo of my father on a trout stream, colonial side tables with a single drawer where she used to keep cartons of red Marlboros and boxes with two aisles of matchbooks—as a kid I used to love the quick flinty smell of sulfur dioxide when she lit up in the car, the window half down. (She smoked so much my brother could steal whole packs and get away with it when getting away with anything was rare.) I brought her a chenille throw blanket from Restoration Hardware that remained folded at the end of her bed. I bought her a little tape player and showed her repeatedly how to use it, even writing the directions on her little notepad, but every time I visited the dust had thickened on Brahms' *Double Concerto* and Mozart's string quartets. When I asked how she was she'd say, "better now," though I hadn't known she was sick and felt bad for not knowing, or simply "I'm fine." I always called before coming and she'd say she wouldn't be there, she had so much packing to do, I wouldn't know where to find her, and I'd say, I'll find you.

Over the next two years she aspirated twice, resulting in pneumonia and midnight ambulances to the ER. I'd race down the Jersey Turnpike from New York, past refineries spewing ochre smoke into the charcoal predawn, under jets descending on Newark airport, green and red lights blinking on the wingtips, listen to rock at loud volumes, and push past the speed limit by twenty or so. Each time they put her through tests, slapped an oxygen mask on her face, left her on a cot in the ER till I negotiated a room. Each time she returned to the skilled nursing, weaker, dreamier, quieter. We wondered if it was enough. Much later a friend of mine confided that at 91, before all the problems began, Chaddy had remarked that she'd had enough but didn't want me to know.

3

My brother and I signed a comfort care policy saying not to hospitalize her again. At 11 one night I got a call from a nurse at the Quadrangle asking me to verify that document. My mom was vomiting and feverish. They'd given her Tylenol and a Z-Pack. Had we said no antibiotics? Where was the document? For an hour I searched mis-filed files in the cellar, locating only her Living Will and mine. My brother in Hawaii finally retrieved his copy and faxed it, a piece of paper with three possibilities, three little lines, three boxes.

- No Antibiotics
- Antibiotics to ensure comfort
- Antibiotics to sustain life.

On a summer afternoon sitting in my backyard, we had checked number two. Was I to tell the nurse, "no more"? I felt like a murderer. "I'll say it," said my brother.

The distinctions between 2 and 3 seemed as hazy as the vapor-simmering horizon along the highway, equivocal as our knowing her life had shrunk to the width of a wheelchair and knowing that her little lashless eyes brightened even momentarily when we arrived.

Her chances were 20% without antibiotics, 50% with. Where does a doctor come up with these numbers? Does he enter age, length of illness, temperature, and blood pressure in a calculator and times it all by some quantity X and—ping!—be alive or not? Had he forgotten what a fighter she was? Had he factored in will, stubbornness, courage? Fear? All these years and I didn't know if she was afraid to die. She surely wasn't going to some pleasant cloud from which she could watch her grandkids get married and continue the line. Donate my organs, she'd said, and she carried a little card in her wallet with instructions. The woman was always prepared. Don't bury me. The thought of it fills me with horror.

0% That's what I knew. No figuring involved. Zero hit me like a fastball in the jaw, and I made the trip again. Fast. There she lay under the Restoration throw, her cheeks just as rosy as they'd always been, but now I guessed it was fever. I laid my hand on her forehead, so warm. She didn't open her eyes. A clear mask covered her face, which tilted upward and to the side. I sat up close on the bed and put my hand on her shoulder. We WASPs aren't demonstrative. We don't touch much. We don't say "love you" at the end of every phone call. I don't think she ever said those words to me, ever. But I told her. Do you hear me?

I heard "my mother is dying, my mother is dying" while I taught classes the next day. The words swam like fish under ice on which I skated the practiced figure eights.

Pokie was by her bed when she died, but I was not. Did she groan, gasp suddenly, sigh? Did Pokie recognize those sounds or were they something altogether new? Did she whisper goodbye to anyone or did she not know she would only breathe an hour more, a minute? Maybe my words about love had alerted her. Cruel words.

Death is a trigger. Death charges inanimate things. Death is war, death is peace. Death is a strand of hair left in a comb after the body is burned. Death is memory. Death is distortion and re-creation, grotesque and exquisite. It is lips moving in your brain. It is giving up trying to hear it.

When I opened the door to her room, cold hit my nose and cheeks. They'd shut off the heat and stripped the bed where she had lain two days before. The oxygen machine stood gawkily in the corner. Her closet burst obscenely with blouses and turtlenecks stretched on plastic hangers, cotton pants, size extra-large to go over diapers, and a bright red blazer with a black velvet collar that she hadn't worn in years. I yanked at the plastic hangers, pulled off the clothes and rolled them up in clumps and stuffed them into garbage bags. I threw in the spanking new Reeboks, a single snow glove, cable-knit sweaters, her heathery purple overcoat, and a crumpled Liberty scarf. To charity.

Then, a box of brown bobby pins still in her drawer after fifty years, a used tissue, dog treats in a jacket pocket. I saw her standing before her bureau holding up a hand mirror to see the back of her hair, flicking the comb to get each curl just right. I saw her toss a biscuit to

Pokie as she left her apartment, lights on, TV on, in case the dog got lonely. Death opens little boxes of useless pins.

Death opens histories, stories told and untold. That's the reason for funerals. Except my mom didn't want one. That may be the ultimate WASP ethos: Oh don't bother. I just died, but don't mind me. Music, I believe, was her religion. At least it lifted her out of her fastidious coping, you could see it on her face. She didn't think much of priests. And all her friends were dead by the time she died.

So I asked my kids to tell me what they remembered most, and I asked my brother, and I read closely for the first time an account her brother Dick wrote about his trip to England to search out the family roots, longing as he was for some claim to aristocracy underlying their long-lost, near-Downton Abbey existence, or to a cousin who might serve as an anchor to the Chadwick-Collins clan orphaned in America since 1920.

Dick wandered a long country lane in Cornwall, searching for Nanscow (Cornish for wooded valley), a dour gray stone house where his great-grandfather, James, had been born. There he found a young farmer couple, who had never heard of the Collins family and probably wondered at my uncle, brazenly knocking on their door. James had left home quite young and started a wool business in Exeter. A picture of him dating from 1860 shows a "tall, well-dressed young man with a pleasant face and a look of quiet desperation." He married Elizabeth Lund, a Viking descendant and great-granddaughter of Sir Andrew Chadwick, who made a fortune in the cotton industry in the 18th century. James and Elizabeth lived in Northernhay house, a mansion in the center of Exeter with grounds of three acres. I went there, too, on a less ambitious foray for my roots. The place is now a public park with rolling lawns and natural English style gardens, the house itself torn down.

Of three phantom houses in our past, I grew up hearing about the last, Howe Lodge in Bournemouth, with its dark secret tunnel to the sea that pirates used to use for smuggling whatever they smuggled. The ivy covered house with crenellated walls dated from the early 19th century. Its morning room opened onto the tennis lawn, which was rolled after every rain by White the head gardener and divided into two courts. Chaddy's parents, James (son of the wool merchant) and Caroline, lived there with a staff whose numbers I can only imagine. Mrs. Wills ruled the large flag-stone paved kitchen, governess Miss Pears lived in a nearby thatched cottage, and a formidable nanny reigned in the nursery, allowing my grandmother to see her kids only at designated hours. My grandparents "dressed" for dinner every evening, meaning it was a black tie event. Caroline, originally from New Orleans, had been studying singing in Paris when James saw her picture on the piano of her teacher and said, "That is the woman I'm going to marry." And so he did, but with an ironic wave of a baton, he blocked her singing career. No wife of his on a stage.

Caroline's mother, Galie, lived at Howe Lodge too. She was a cousin of General Beauregard, the army officer who issued the order to fire on Fort Sumpter in 1860, thereby starting the Civil War. James's imperious mother also moved in, and Dick says she hated him. "I was scrawny and bad tempered and when she thought I had misbehaved, she came after me with a stick, so I would hide in the bushes."

James was "in the military" and basically never worked. He did manage to lose the fortune, which was the impetus to emigrate. Parents and three children (Chaddy then age three), along with Galie and a young farm girl, Eva, set sail in 1920. They all lived in a little house on Railroad Avenue in Bryn Mawr because Caroline went to work at the college. When Dick tried to visit Howe Lodge in the '70s, only the cellars remained. Council houses had replaced the stable block and the walled garden was a parking lot.

Thoroughly uprooted, he wrote: "So the family looks forward to growth and prosperity in the New World—not often living our dreams but trying as best as we can to give a sample of our best."

Like water spiraling in ever smaller circles before vanishing, family histories shrink, individual possibility narrows. Chaddy moved from the family house in Bryn Mawr where she lived for fifty years to an independent apartment to assisted living to skilled nursing to a wheelchair. Yesterday I was searching for snow boots and found a box, roughly 6x10 inches, tucked under a rose scarf. Auer Cremation Services. It's Christmas time and my husband had put her there, out of sight, for now.

But no. At night memories of her dance in my mind like dandelion fluff or encircle me like a swarm of bees. Death is a floodgate, opening too much too fast. I see her in the style with which my grown son sets the table for dinner. I see her in a yellow blouse and penny loafers on the terrace with me, age ten, the day she decided to tell me about sex. I hear her mother when my daughter sings opera. No, Chaddy didn't live her dreams. Over one of those wine dinners she remarked that after fifty years of marriage she didn't know what my father thought of her. But as a kid I never knew, and I'm grateful. She kicked him under the table, after all, and maintained the status quo. She came from an explosive line, a fiery line of Vikings and Generals, and in later years she targeted me with inexplicable anger. Maybe she explained it all to Pokie, who now lies asleep here with me, in one of the chairs from the old house. Maybe she left the lights on for her for good reason.

Water on Fire

My father pushed back his dining room chair, lit a Camel non-filter, and told me a story, the only one I remember him telling. He was an intelligence officer on an aircraft carrier in the southwest Pacific during World War II. One afternoon he decided not to go down to his quarters to rest but remained on deck. That was the afternoon Japanese subs torpedoed the ship, sending missiles right into my father's bunk. The craft caught fire, and hundreds of men raced from below as gas tanks exploded. With the order to abandon ship, some guys slid down ropes and burned their hands; my father opted to jump, leaping 65 feet into shark-infested water. For some reason, in the following weeks I kept picturing those hands rubbed raw. And it dawned on me that if my father hadn't *happened* to remain on deck that day, *I* wouldn't exist. This was a novel idea for a seven year old—and deep, I thought.

He told the story in his tweed suit and bow tie, probably after a few glasses of good Bordeaux, though I didn't notice at the time. He told it with little inflection against a backdrop of chintz curtains drawn across a wall of windows, bordered by a stone window seat filled with schefleura, African violets, and orchids.

Although my father died twenty-four years ago, only recently did I find four letters he wrote to my mother from Iwo Jima and Okinawa and from the aircraft carrier *Wasp*. He dated the letters by month and day but excluded the year, so I don't know how long he'd been out there when he wrote, "Believe it or not, we have movies every night. It seems about the crowning irony to sit here and watch movies while thousands of young kids are shuddering in icy foxholes and dodging mortar shells a few city blocks away, but on the other hand, why not.

9

It is relaxing, and maybe it helps us to do a better job during the daytime." The letter was typed single-spaced on pale green onion-skin. The comma after "hand" was added in ink, so he proofread his letters, even over there. My father felt the bizarre juxtaposition of events just as I now realize the incongruity of his narrative in the quiet dining room of his stone house on the Main Line. Something in our faintly analogous perceptions moves me, and I keep looking for clues. Especially now that I know his story had nothing to do with me.

Maybe we all had him wrong. My father-in-law, a jazz musician, met my father for the first time on the night before my wedding. His only comment was, "That's one nervous cat." As I grew up, my mother would complain to me about his lack of social ease. She didn't think he quite had it, not like her brothers who spent their early child-hoods in England and went on to Princeton. Furthermore, she wanted him to be strong, to fight back when they argued. Did she know the man who wrote to her, "Every evening at about dusk we would get some enemy planes around, sometimes quite a few. They didn't seem to know their business very well, however, and we got quite used to them. I slept through several air raids very comfortably. It seemed about the most sensible thing to do."

Clearly my father was a man of reason. Although he once had aspirations to write, he decided to practice law—maybe because he turned twenty-one during the Great Depression, maybe because his father and a whole ancestral line behind him had been lawyers, may-be because he'd had polio as a kid and was sent away from home for a year to recuperate. I can only speculate because he never mentioned much passion for anything except the law and trout fishing. All day Sunday he'd sit with a legal pad on his lap editing documents with an even hand. He told me law was like chess, you had to imagine every possible future move; he never said it was like war, but now I see it was. He was more comfortable untangling legalese than throw-ing a baseball to his son, a feat he simply couldn't do. Spilling coffee grounds with abandon, hammering his fingers, banging his head, he was not one with the physical world—except when he pulled on his waders, held up a Cahill to the light to thread it with a fine leader, and cast his fly rod. Back and forth the yellow line swished so slowly and uniformly it seemed suspended in air and time before unfurling at the flick of his wrist along a ruffled stream long and straight into a dark pool by the bank. With unusual candor he told me once that when he couldn't fall asleep at night he'd envision the path—every root, dip, and patch of moss—along his favorite stream where he went as a kid and later took us. And so I smiled when I read in his letter from Iwo Jima, "I have had a chance to meet a few of our rescued aviators. One of them, as a matter of fact, is sleeping in my bunk this minute. He came aboard here for further transfer and was pretty bushed by his experience, which happened yesterday. He was rescued many miles from here, under pretty hectic circumstances and seems very grateful to be alive. It is really wonderful to have such tangible results from our work. Sort of like catching a large trout, only even better." No, my father was not trivializing the event. But I'll never know if "hectic circumstances" was his characteristic understatement or an effort to protect my mother. He was a chauvinist of sorts.

He never described the tough decisions he must have had to make, just as in later years he rarely discussed the law with my mother, intelligent as she was. Nor were these letters of passion so much as snapshots of touristic or anthropological import. Of Okinawa he wrote, "Aside from the dust the island is as pleasant a place as you would want to see. The southern part is gently rolling, and intensively cultivated in many tiny little fields, each bordered with a little retaining wall or a hedgerow. Sugar, rice, barley and sweet potatoes seem to be what they are growing, in case you are interested." (I can't imagine that she was, under the circumstances.) "Also many goats and ponies. The houses are of two kinds, thatched roof and tile roof. Otherwise they are the same small square structures with flimsy lattice and plaster walls. Very snug and quaint looking, and filthy beyond belief inside. The Okinawans lived very closely with their animals. What makes their settlements particularly unattractive is the fact that they apparently do not rely solely on animal manure to provide a source of fertilizer." Normally, my father was not one for extra words, especially adverbs, nor euphemisms, which he basically thought were an insult to the English language. It seems he needed to be a gentleman for his Main Line bride, but what underlay such objective reporting? What footing, what rocky streambed, was he navigating unseen? He went on to say, "After an Okinawan dies, he spends the next three years sitting up. He is placed in a part of the vault in a sitting position and there he sits for three years, decomposing for all he is worth. After that the bones are collected and placed in extremely beautiful urns, and there he stays presumably until the end of time." Was he being facetious giving the dead man agency over his own decay? I think he was intrigued, whether or not my mother would be.

When I was eight, my father decided we were going to Nassau in July, by car. In a black Falcon wagon with no air conditioning, my brother and I in the back with the back seat down, romping about, playing War and Go Fish and Crazy 8's while sucking on Sugar Daddies that never seemed to end, we chugged through blistering southern states, stopping at slow diners and segregated water fountains, all because my father had developed a fear of flying in the war. "From up there you looked down at a postage stamp," he said, "and just prayed you'd find it." I didn't think much about the fear, maybe because fathers weren't supposed to feel it, or maybe because later he got over it and flew all over the globe, rhapsodizing about the Concord to Paris. But prayers didn't get my father through the war. It was a strange figure of speech for one who never went to church and swore he wanted no service whatsoever at his death. He wrote to my mother from the carrier: "My other room mate is the ship's Chaplain, and a complete joker in my opinion. He passes out little pamphlets and cards, with inspirational messages in or on them. Just before D-Day, every officer was presented with a little card which contained something on it called 'Prayer before going into Battle', and it was in my opinion the ultimate in corn. In the first place I can't quite figure out how he concluded that we, sitting here on this safe comfortable ship, were 'going into battle' just because we were near enough to be eyewitnesses of the marines' ordeal. And in the second place the whole idea revolted me. He is horribly friendly, too. Whenever he meets anybody he immediately says 'What is your home state?' This is enough to end the conversation immediately. At least it was in my case."

My father disliked sentimentality and disingenuous displays of emotion as much as he did euphemisms. I was a teenager in the '60s when poet Gary Snyder and the like were telling men to exhibit feeling and stop being so uptight. My father was repressed, we said; he had no vocabulary for his emotions, if he had them at all. My mother told me she was worried that I thought he didn't love me because he never, ever said those words. And long after that Florida trip, when I was old enough to know that fathers feel fear, he said nothing when I cracked a vertebra in my neck. Halfway around the world, I leapt from my boyfriend's shoulders into water that was suddenly too shallow. As I emerged from the water, my arms and legs were shaking convulsively. I downed two scotches and decided against a Balinese doctor. On I went to Sumatra, to Thailand, by myself, riding a rickety bus at night from Bangkok to Chiang Mai. Only three weeks later did x-rays reveal my near paralysis. It didn't sink in. I simply wanted to take off the hideous neck brace. My mother took me to doctors and plied them with questions. At home, my father looked at me—and shuddered. Though I recall the twinge of his shoulders vividly and quick shivery syllables from his lips as if he'd stepped into the Arctic, it has taken years to appreciate what they meant, to fill in what he never said.

When I read his few words of passion to my mother at the end of each letter, I felt strangely proud of him. "No mail for several days. I don't know what happened to the service. It stinks. Just the same, though, it is damn nice to know that when it does come there will be letters from you. Nice passionate ones, I hope." I suppose he never knew for sure, and the hope just dangled there over the South Pacific. They hadn't known each other long when he went to war. Engaged by telegram, he came home for a two-week leave; they said their vows and he went back to sea. When I was growing up, the most visible emotion I witnessed was his reluctance to make her angry; I say reluctance because it wasn't exactly fear. As with chess, the law, and the war, he had to anticipate.

In this vein he narrated in one letter the fate of a few pairs of socks: "I think I neglected to break the sad news to you that some time ago a room-boy sent my bag to the laundry before I had a chance to remove from same a large number of those good woolen socks produced by you and your mother, which I had temporarily parked in the laundry bag. The results were just as you would expect them to be. I doubt if even young Carol [my infant cousin] could have got her foot into one of them when they came back from the laundry. The result is that I have only a few pairs of woolens left. And I don't want you to think for a minute that this is a hint." But of course it was. Even then he tread as gingerly around her as in a minefield on Iwo Jima. Such proper legal language—"from same"—and such proclaimed innocence! As if he ever would have thought to take dirty socks out of the bag!

Whether or not he failed to foresee the room-boy, he definitely failed to gauge my mother on at least one occasion. In a long letter whose first page is mysteriously missing, he struggled to quell the anger he somehow had ignited. "In view of the difficulties of corresponding across thousands of miles," he wrote at the top of page 2, "how about giving old Sutton the benefit of a few doubts." Clearly he thought she should since he didn't end the sentence with a question mark, careful editor though he was. What could have kindled her fury? A remark about a sexy actress in one of the movies he saw? What would lead her to interrogate someone she loved, already besieged by bombers halfway around the world? Most of his reply resorts to objective reporting on the beauties of Okinawa, the pointed hills surmounted by jutting craggy rocks full of caves, the palmettos, banana trees, giant ferns, and bamboo. "A botanist would go nuts," he wrote (effectively distancing himself); "So would a landscape painter." My mother decided to keep this part, innocuous as it was, but I see her crumpling his allusion to the festering topic and hurling it in the trash. She even took a pencil to the final page, scribbling zigzags in the margins and around his closing "all my love," like a kid testing a new crayon that she can only hold in her fist. At length and only under duress, he wrote words I could never have imagined him saying: "Keep young and healthy and beautiful for me, and the next time I make some stupid blunder in one of my letters just try to remember that in my erratic fashion I love you more than anything in the world and want your happiness more than anything I can think of. Say this to yourself about twenty times before writing a reply, and then if you are still mad at me, sit down and really give me hell." If she did, I'll never know. Her answer, written by hand with great loops and pronounced crossing of Ts, bearing feelings of hurt incarnate as hot red anger, would have exploded, shredded, and dissolved into silent syllables on the dark floor of the Pacific as the *Wasp* slowly went down. But his words on the page lie in my hand like pirate treasure. His heartfelt wishes for her, his declaration of love, his love like deep sea pearls.

I can't help noting, though, that it is only after such fluid eloquence, with its parallel sentiments, coupled with a rare admission of error that he, ever the strategist, is willing to take her on.

I scour these surviving letters for the man I called "Daddy," who only told me one story and became Pop (like his father) after my children were born. I'm no longer growing up, and my search is not about my childhood or me. I arrive at the question, Why do we want to remember someone—anyone? I feel a pull like the tug of a riptide to know who he was, for *his* sake, though he's not watching from heaven, we can both be sure, and for ill-defined reasons that make the dead as real or unreal as the living.

I search for the man who shuddered, the man who, I begin to see, felt more than he revealed, so carefully did he balance his appreciation of the terrors around him with lucid rationality about what needed to be done. From Iwo Jima he wrote: "I went to sleep last night to the accompaniment of intermittent dynamiting by the Marines of the caves in Mount Suribachi. It is a queer way to go to sleep and just one of the things that makes this existence seem so [so added in pen] unreal. This morning when I woke up they were still blasting away. The Japs have dozens of caves in the mountain, all interconnected by tunnels, we hear, and they no doubt have rations to hold out more or less indefinitely. One wonders whether eventually the Marines will seal up all the caves. A gruesome but fairly practical solution. (Remember Poe's "The Cask of Amontillado"?)

I feel the restraint in his words "a queer way to go to sleep" like a heartbeat under my palm that I can't hear. Tell me. Queer, not ordinary, what then? What did you imagine? Did you put a pillow over your head in the dead of night? Did you muffle the explosions, dream them far away? To call the scene "unreal," and even, as an after thought, "so unreal," is comfortingly vague—no cause for alarm to my mother—and yet I see through those four letters as through the porthole of his carrier to a man chilled by his dislocation, his distance from home, and the ironic juxtaposition of sleep and violence. For my father, "so unreal" was loaded because he thought he could create and control his reality and had evidence to defend his case; if he worked, he could be editor-in-chief of Penn's Law Review, which he was; if he performed consistently, he could climb the corporate ladder at his firm, which he did. But this war unleashed his imagination, spiraling him out of reality and into fiction where, through quiet parenthetical allusion, he let the macabre mind of Poe paint the pictures he saw but refused to write himself, though he might have. And despite the word "remember" I somehow doubt my mother knew the story, much less ever discussed it with him. Perhaps this was his way of suggesting she read it. Read him.

In the same letter my father wrote, "For the first few days we were here we wheeled slowly around the island at what seemed like fairly close range to me, kind of tempting the Japs to shoot at us—a temptation which they did not always resist. One or two big ones landed fairly close to us while I was watching, and I don't know how many others while I was below…. The ships that amazed me were the little mine sweeps who were tooting around within absolute spitting distance of the beach right from the very start. For some reason or other they didn't seem to get pasted, perhaps because the Japs didn't want to give away their gun positions for such small game. Nevertheless I do not hanker to have duty on a minesweep."

As an officer did he think the carrier was really too close to shore— in which case I think he would have told my mother the exact distance, and the distance he would have advised—or did it *feel* that way, especially after two "big ones" landed close by? It "seemed" pretty close—which *must* have been disturbing—and he admitted the subjectivity of his perception in the simple phrase "to me." The last two understated sentences of the paragraph betray two voices battling within: though he deduced a reason why the Japanese didn't "paste" those minesweeps, he was afraid to be on one.

When a pack of submarines took his "safe, comfortable ship" by surprise, my father flattened himself on deck and, reportedly, did not entertain the idea of imminent death. "I was wondering what you did with a lighted cigarette when bombs are dropping."

I found this comment in a torn clipping from the *Philadelphia Inquirer,* folded five times among the letters, umber and frail as a beech leaf in December. Titled "Philadelphian Describes Sinking of Wasp After Submarine Attack," the article features a portrait of my father in jacket and tie looking lawyerly, his hair combed back above deep-set eyes, his thin lips composed. Adjacent is a cartoon sketch of an officer being hurtled toward us in a blast of light and sailors in undershirts behind him looking helplessly upward. There's a photo of the ship in the distance, smoke pouring from deck and hull, bow to stern, beyond the blurred figures of men on the destroyer from which the picture was taken. In another shot Captain Forrest Sherman, the commanding officer who made the decision to abandon ship, bows his head.

Reporter Frederic Hyde opens the piece in a romantic vein, a voice so different from my father's: "Here is the story of two thousand men who took a boat ride a third of the way around the world looking for trouble—and how they found it.

"They were the men of the airplane carrier *Wasp,* the fighting crew of a great ship which met her gallant and helpless end while carrying the war to the Japanese in the Southwest Pacific. She and they had a job to do, and they did it."

He then introduces my father: "One of them, talking as matter-of-factly as though jumping 65 feet from the fiery, slanted deck of a sinking ship into shark-infested waters were part of the day's routine, told me the story upon his return to his home in Philadelphia. He is Lieut. James A. Sutton, of 5409 Overbrook Avenue.... These are the last hours of the *Wasp* as he remembers them:"

As I look for Daddy's words in the text that follows, I'm confounded. Hyde's introduction would indicate the entire story to come is what my father told, verbatim, and yet he quotes him directly midway through the narrative, thereby distinguishing the other rhetoric as his own. I'll never know for sure which words were his, just as I knew more of him through what my mother said than what he ever said to me.

As my father via Hyde tells it, on September 15, 1942, the *Wasp* and a convoy of transports and freighters were bringing men and guns to reinforce the Marines and soldiers on Guadalcanal. The carrier's job was to protect the slower ships from attack by the Japanese who were on their way to intercept them. Pilots took off early that morning, fanning out hundreds of miles ahead of the ship and scanning the sea for subs. By noon they reported bombing a Kawanishi flying boat that was lumbering along almost within sighting distance of the *Wasp*. Since the Kawanishi may have had time to radio that it was under attack by carrier type planes, Sherman issued an order for radio silence. Just after noon another batch of fighters and scout bombers went up, some that never returned, while others were brought below to the hangar deck for refueling. At that point the loudspeakers boomed, "the smoking light is out," which meant no smoking below because of the gas.

Mid-afternoon my father was in the central structure that rises above the flight deck. "I'd left some of the pilots in the ready room about 2:30," he reported, "after relaying them some new instructions. They seemed edgy and didn't talk much. There wasn't any of the usual rough-housing. They acted as if they'd much rather have been aloft." He was in touch with the mood of his men, this man who didn't know a thing about emotion.

"I was about to go back to the quarters I shared with another junior officer, and had lit a cigarette. Then it happened.

"Wham! There was a terrific explosion with the sound of metal going through metal, like a million furnace doors slamming shut all at once."

"The deck heaved as though there had been an earthquake. The ports of the island structure were blacked out, so I couldn't see outside, but they told me afterward a sheet of flame flared up on the starboard side 100 feet into the air." Then he must have hurried out on deck.

"Ten seconds later, we got it again. Our first thought was that we were under air attack. We dropped on the deck, flattened ourselves out, and waited for the next one." In that moment he wondered about his lit cigarette and mashed it out on deck.

My father was only 5 foot 8 ½ inches (he never omitted the half) and probably didn't weigh more than 140. I picture him lying like a matchstick on the roiling deck, ruminating on the next course of action and never losing his cool. To me, he didn't say much about what followed, but he told Hyde that a few minutes later a heavier explosion occurred somewhere deep in the ship. Smoke poured out of the hatchway from the hangar deck and men came swarming up the ladders into open air. The ship was pitched like a roof, and all lights went out below as gas tanks in the standing planes blew up one after another. The pumps were blasted, leaving no water in the fire hose. Destroyers raced alongside dropping depth bombs, and ammunition aboard planes on the forward deck exploded.

At that point the men calmly took off their shoes, put on life jackets and abandoned ship, just as my father had told me when I was seven. He held his nose and closed his eyes and leapt. "Jumping from the stern ramp," he said to Hyde, "you wonder whether you're ever going to hit." How long are moments of free fall from a six-story building through deafening air? So long he didn't think about the landing but only *if* he would land. So long he had time to speculate about what he couldn't anticipate. He hadn't told me when I was young that blazing oil covered the water around the ship, that some were caught in it and died. Instead he'd told me about the sharks, and I always pictured his legs dangling helplessly there as he wondered what lurked below. But I was wrong.

"Sharks? I don't believe anybody thought about them," my father told Hyde. "I know I didn't. The oil was worse. You couldn't help swallowing some of the stuff. And it was awfully indigestible."

After a destroyer picked him up a day later, he ate a sandwich, drank some coffee and went to sleep while U.S. ships torpedoed the *Wasp* and finished her off. To the end he concealed as irrelevant what he must have felt, conceding only an upset stomach, of all things—as if commenting on a steak in a disappointing restaurant. That was the Daddy I knew, but of course he wouldn't have said even that in the middle of dinner. He was too polite but, no, not uptight. "A bit tough," he might have admitted a day later.

My father went back to sea on another carrier. He spent three more years out there, returning from duty physically unscathed. During the winter of '45 he went sledding and broke his nose. Before I knew the meaning of irony, I felt it when Daddy told me that (with a quick smile and a shrug). His prominent nose remained slightly crooked for the rest of his life.

The Fly in the Refrigerator

Late last night I opened the fridge in a dark kitchen. As fluorescent light dazzled my eyes and I squinted for the leftover pie, a huge blue fly torpedoed the butter. I swatted blindly, it buzzed louder, spiraling across day-old salad, sticky rims of lemonade on the foggy top shelf, wildly aware of the bonanza at hand but unable to rest with me fanning at it and shouting oh my god. That fly was at the right place at the right time, that is, if you can assume that *someone* would have needed to eat *something* in the ensuing hours and released it before it grew numb in a fleck of spilled juice wondering, if a fly could, if it had been worth it. At the moment a feast stood ready. Bristling and ablaze, it zigzagged between the light and me until I cupped my palm and ushered it out into the night.

Recalling her death (before death), Emily Dickinson describes a very still room where family have gathered, cried, and now stand waiting, where she the body awaits *something*, yes, there *must* be something.... She listens. Buzz. A fly veers between the light and her. Such positioning! Such essentially right positioning to disabuse her of any intimation of godhead, any key to the ultimate enigma, in her final hour. Who else would dare? Who would say that truth trumps illusion, even then, when it could hardly matter, or perhaps matter more than ever? Left with uncertain stumbling buzzing, the poet dies. The fly remains obliviously alive. Maybe it lands on her cold knuckles crossed over her chest or spins out a crack in the window to new orbs of horse manure in a nearby field. Being in the wrong place at the wrong time, it had the final word even if God had the first.

Our fly wound up not on a life supply of butter but in our bedroom zooming around our reading lights and crashing into walls. I breathed, I tried to focus. Transcend, I told myself, reading about a mom whose baby had kidney cancer, a mom who said you just don't say baby and cancer in the same sentence. It was the jagged unpredictability of the fly that I couldn't stand, its sudden kamikaze flights past my nose, inside the lampshade, thwack. Brian, you've got to get that fly. Why me? It's a guy thing, I said, wincing, be the hunter. He bit, skeptically, and lumbered out of bed to find a fly swatter. We needed a strategy. I turned on the porch light, opened the screen door, shut off my light and waited. Nothing. No sound except the September katydids, chirruping still with thinning voices, recalling for me the fullness of summer and the slip of water against my skin. I flicked on my light, which resurrected the fly. It peeled out from under my bed somewhere and danced toward the bathroom light where Brian caught it in the wrong place (for the fly) and, being a man (but not God) smacked it dead.

The night we moved into our house, my mind jibed like the berserk flight of that fly. It was Memorial Day weekend, 104 degrees, our windows flung open and hot air hanging on the trees like guilt. Motorcycles ripped up the hill, teenagers in convertibles ground the gears and whooped at freedom, just around the bend. My baby cried, again. 2:14 a.m. I left the sweat-soaked sheet and went to get her, groping for the light switch and hearing the unfamiliar creak of wood underfoot, I having little more idea where I was than she, just two weeks old and learning to cry for food and comfort and human touch. I sat in an old armchair whose springs were shot, nursing her, hoping she didn't hear the hoots and roars outside. Why was I here instead of the apartment in the city where the spin of tires and sporadic car alarm were the norm, where heels clicked and voices came home from wine bars, talking earnestly about non-earnest things? Why was I listening to the ticking trudge of the grandfather clock that used to be in the house where I grew up? For a moment the traffic ceased, as if the whole world had exhaled and waited for its heartbeat to slow. Then headlights beamed through the room, throwing shadow bars of the crib against the opposite wall for an instant before leaving only the pink hush of the night light from beside my chair. My baby swallowed, her lids slowly closed, her tiny fingers found my T-shirt, her fists were soft plums.

For months the big house was empty since we couldn't afford furniture. The dining room had a playpen instead of a table, the living room a ragged palm tree and wicker couch bought second hand. It's *cold*, my parents said that torrid summer. Get some curtains.

During the first week I found empty beer bottles on the back terrace, which we hadn't used. And one afternoon my three year old tumbled off a slide and got a knee full of gravel. As I bent over the rim of the bathtub gingerly dabbing with a washcloth to unwedge the grit while Paul screamed and shoved my hand, the baby slept in a pram in the kitchen downstairs. Needing to buy a bandage and tape, I came downstairs and found that my pocketbook, which I'd slung over the handles of the pram, was gone. I searched closets, beds, doorknobs where I might have hung it, the car. In the bushes ten feet up the street lay my wallet—disengorged—which *had* been on Sophia's pram *while she slept.*

I told my husband we should move. He said they caught the guy, he just wanted drug money, and this house was the best deal we could've gotten, and we could use the public schools, and he had a good commute, and it was a stretch but the right thing to do. I doubt he ever loved the house, but he planted futile grass seed and painted the exterior and re-did the crumbling terrace nonetheless, thereby making my wrong house a little more right.

We came to refer to it as the fortress, a bulky stucco house high enough to survive rising water levels as polar ice caps dissolve, its walls thick enough to retain heat in winter from clanking radiators and deflect intense sunlight in summer, a house where we raised two stocky kids who have positioned themselves in the world, solidly. Despite all this concrete fortitude, this place, like any other, is fluid. Someone asked me the other day if I'd ever been happy—really happy—which I suppose entails a desire to be only where one is, not awaiting divine epiphany (with unwarranted certainty) or remembering your baby's first laugh (with nostalgia).

I admitted to this person, yes, silly as it seems, there was a day. The kitchen table was littered with strips of construction paper. Neon green glue, thick magic markers and cups of lemonade covered the pumpkin orange counter tops, hideous counter tops we had vowed to replace a few years back. The black and white floor tiles were gritty underfoot, and the puppy shredded the paper we dropped. It was late afternoon.

"Mom!" yelled Sophie, then three, up on a chair in front of a sink overflowing with bubbles. The sprayer nozzle dangled over the side, dripping onto the floor while water doggedly advanced across the counters in all directions. "It's getting full," she commented with uncharacteristic understatement, looking at me with impish eyes, her rose dress soaked across her belly. Paul was at the kitchen table meticulously selecting the right colored pencil from an array of 100. His sandy hair, long and home cut, fell over his eyes, and he kept flicking it back as he filled every white space on that paper. Beside him were *The Red Knight* and *The Mad Scientist and the Fish*, construction paper books with spines the length of two staples. We were renovating my old dollhouse—a two-story, classic colonial, the kind I would've liked to live in, with a spacious kitchen, a fireplace, and a bathroom the size of the bedrooms. We'd painted the exterior bright yellow with turquoise trim and splashed the gray roof with pink. As a kid I never liked the dollhouse much. Friends would come over and rearrange all the furniture while I just wanted to go outside. But that afternoon, with Peter, Paul, and Mary crooning about flowers and the warm kitchen oozing hominess, I didn't want to go anywhere. I'm sure there were many afternoons like that. But that's the one I remember, the definitive one.

Sometimes the feeling of essential rightness is simply wrong. Recently my daughter (now twenty-six) left work early, rushed to get the subway from Lincoln Center to Riverdale, and pushed her way onto the 1 train, thinking it was the 2 or 3. When she got to 96th, she wriggled past wedged bodies, muttering to passengers that she had to get out. She dashed to the train across the platform, smiling, ahead of schedule. But when the train rumbled east, jolting and hiccupping rather than speeding northward, Sophie texted, *I totally fucked up.* At the next stop she got out, crossed the platform, *shit this is not funny,* descended, got on another train and went back to 96th where the platform was more crowded than she'd seen it in five years of living in New York. *I'll never get on, it's packed.* The doors opened, crowds swarmed in, sweating, heaving, leaning. With a wall of people before her and doors about to close—she hurled herself against three broad women as someone shrieked, "There's a baby inside!" Sophie rode to 256th, bewildered by how she could have been so sure the wrong place was the right one and the right one, wrong.

Maybe a crowd was pouring in, and she'd gone along with a sense of collective purpose. Maybe a phone call or headache had upended her sense of direction, making habit illusory and misleading. I always take this subway, it must be right. Or maybe it was timing, pure and simple, like marrying the candidate who arrives when the moment seems opportune. Did the train whine to a halt or did she glance up out of boredom or feel an uneasy inkling as random as the buzz of an errant fly? Recognition! Something drove Oedipus to grill the messenger, something compelled him to discover he had definitely been in the wrong place at the wrong time and killed the king despite tortuous plans not to. Every attempt not to fulfill his fate proved as futile and trifling as a moth flapping at a lit windowpane. My daughter didn't intend to get in the wrong train; a fly didn't intend to make a mockery of a poet, or God.

Unlike Oedipus and his tragic trajectory, Sophie could return and undo, though the crowd was hostile, the air hot and scarce. She reached 256th Street where I picked her up, and we headed east on the Cross Island and L.I.E. By then we were an hour behind schedule, but we'd missed most of rush hour traffic so we made up time. I don't subscribe to the idea that everything happens for a reason, or that anything is meant to happen. Nevertheless, her error was not entirely inopportune, which blurred even slightly our definitive calculation of right and wrong.

The other day I emerged from a subway and blithely strode three blocks before I realized I was walking north though it felt *so* south. Yes, I have a lousy sense of direction but such dizzy disorientation gets one thinking. Maybe a wrong decision that felt right hurtled me down rails that forked and forked again as irreparably as time leaves tracks on my skin. Where should I have stopped, gotten off, looked around and at which stop would I have called the wrong turn a mistake or an unavoidable detour or the essential journey? These retrospective constructs make a museum of the past, which was never fixed in time, just as frozen portraits surround a dying poet while her very being is reduced to a fly (taking corkscrew dives at a light).

Eclipsed

My husband says solar thermal technology traps the sun's heat with mirrors to power electrical generators, and Germany is building a photovoltaics power plant the size of two hundred soccer fields... he claims that China will have five million electric cars on its roads by 2020. Such facts slide off his tongue over dinner on a Monday night. He does the *New York Times* crossword religiously and rapidly. He knows stuff. On December 20 Brian confided (with a tentative glance in my direction), "The moon hasn't done this since 1638. I'm setting an alarm."

"Good idea," I chirped, having no intention of getting up. I entered my daughter's room and quietly closed the door. The knob didn't work, no latch to click and catch. I felt like the bad wife, the betrayer, but the limpid blue quilt and linen curtains quivering over the radiator, the Hendrix poster that used to be mine, and velvet silence seduce me every time. What is his crime? He breathes: not the silent angelic inhalations of my daughter but the determined seizing of air of a man who makes things happen, followed by fluttery exhalations whispering quiet defeats of which I'm unaware. This labor is all too mortal, too contrived. Like doing Pilates or jogging to live longer. Starkly awake, I can't not count each breath, which is tricky at an age when I might count the years and calculate how many remain before I sit in a wheelchair in a trance of things done and undone, as my mother presently does. I bury my head under a pillow or flee to my daughter's bed, she having grown and left.

Earlier that night, my husband out, I stood in the backyard watching a fat white moon rise over the peaks of my neighbor's house. The surface swelled and shone like mother-of-pearl skin stretched taut. I remembered my midwife, who claimed the maternity ward always overflowed on nights of a full moon. Gravitational pull, she had said.

My daughter had stayed high in the uterus, showing no signs of making an entrance long past the time when the medical world said she should. Two weeks late, two extra weeks growing plump in the dark, dreaming dreams without context, she descended when the moon waxed full, winking at her birth, two hours before a scheduled caesarean.

I woke up sweating. The Tensor light was on, my computer open on my lap. I still wore a hooded sweatshirt over a thin shirt, damp across the chest. With an immense force of will I clunked the computer onto the floor, swept the covers from my legs and yanked at the sweatshirt. 3:23 glowed from the pink alarm clock. Why undress? In a semi-dream I realized with greater acuity than before that the moon was doing something strange or the earth was doing something to the moon that it hadn't in four centuries, and I should witness what that was because it wouldn't happen again for another eighty or so years, which might as well be four hundred. So I pulled on some jeans and padded past the gaping dark of our room, from which long low soughing arose from a swaddled form. He must have seen it, I thought. He had a plan, and he is a man who follows through. Down the stairs I went, not even waking the dog, threw on a parka and hat and boots and unlocked the front door and stepped down the bluestone steps we'd laid a few years ago when Brian decided to renovate.

The moon had freed itself from bristling oaks and a wire cage straddling the neighbor's chimney to the east, crossed the sky, and now posed blood orange over the Hudson. Straight black limbs stretched toward it, twitching slightly. In the hours I had inadvertently slept, it had shrunk, aged, receded. Shadows like wet stones mottled one side, but the other gleamed, a dazzling, painful red. Moon without sun. Sinister and spectacular and alone. I should wake him, he should see this, maybe he has, I can't talk about this. Eye wide open, as if the night would consume it alive—deep red eye burning into mine, radiating a splash of needles from the pupil at its core. Nearly lightless, nearly deathless. Stone and crater, crater and stone. I closed my fists in my pockets, tensed the muscles in my thighs, breathed sharp scallops of air, and tried to swallow four hundred years in a gulp. The moon needed no reason, and I had no explanation.

The earth, that was it, the earth's particles, Brian had explained. I would ask him in the morning, if I let on that I had seen it. But he must have . . . I nearly believed. And if not, what vision would he have missed?

Wrapping the star-pricked sky around me, stamping the auburn eye in my mind with the conviction of never forgetting—as if one could remember such things as your baby's first sound or the remote look in her eyes under neon light and bodies looming like planets above, big and amorphous and unexplained. Would she see the moon smoldering red in eighty years? Or would her daughters? Or would they, missing her, wish she had seen such a sight? Those shadows spreading like smoke over the lovely orange face of the moon were absurdly sad and heroic. Especially on this day that had to happen for this effect to occur, this day of least light of the year in the northern hemisphere when people used to entreat the sun to return and now simply assume it will. I thought of my mother sleeping deeply in her hospital room, on her back, her new floral nightgown open at the neck in the over-heated room where she sits all day, nodding involuntarily and sleeping while light dreams tumble in her mind, letting her believe her mother will pick her up and take her home the next day, but each waking day grows shorter, and she worries that she has not packed. I thought of the confluence of eyes on this climactic moon and of cloud-covered countries that would see computer images after the fact and be satisfied and of millions sleeping unaware that for a meticulously recorded few hours the moon was struggling to glow like graffiti in a subway tunnel. Was my standing in the street in the heart of the night a lie? Without him I would not be there. But to wake him, to kiss him, would break the spell. Alternatively, as the fairy tale goes, the spoiled princess throws her frog against a wall in disgust, or lets him sleep on her pillow all night. Either way, through violence or sex, sex and violence, presto, she has her prince. She didn't even have to believe.

Dark blotches backlit by orange were encroaching on the moon's blushing face as I stood there, guilty and alive, not knowing how long was long enough and not knowing much more than those who saw such a moon in the centuries preceding 1638 and not knowing if omission constitutes betrayal any less than does an eclipse of the one you love.

Where was the sun-lit moon hanging over a mountain in Wyoming that I saw when I was fifteen, alone and virginal, two thousand miles from home, sitting on a sandstone ledge and squinting at the silver light (or at the fact) that a man in a high-tech suit was bounding over her surface insensible to her gravity, reporting data to earth, and implanting an immortal flag? That hour was well before the shared life—when unrecorded nights with someone were the stuff of dreams, and you believed that someone, like a shadow betraying the missing part of a quarter moon, was needed to complete you.

Everyone I knew (and a boy in New Hampshire I didn't yet know) watched Armstrong take the historic step in black and white, marveling as much at the fact that they could watch from a couch in the den as at the completion of the mission that Kennedy had promised "before this decade is out." The moment was thrillingly irreversible and American. But something quivered down my spine and tugged like a plumb bob dropped too fast. On my perch above a field and gleaming stream, enveloped in the scent of cedars and dry rock cooled quickly after sunset, loss seeped like blood from a rite of passage whose meaning I could not understand.

In forty years I scarcely thought of that night, recalled it in flickers and starts, maybe, behind wars in Vietnam and Iraq, behind love and childbirth, which eclipsed it.

Brazen moon! Bit of slow burning coal in the sky tonight!

My legs led me up the stone steps, and my jacket fell on a kitchen chair. Without a light I went softly upstairs, re-passed my bedroom door too cold to wake him and explain, and heard only my distant breathing as I closed the door on unspoken moments and slid between sheets, pulled the morning blue comforter over my shoulders and hugged my daughter's floppy lamb. Had I not slept I would have heard the alarm an hour later, but no footsteps and no door.

If the earth were not cloaked in air, the moon would have merely turned black in its shadow and re-emerged unblemished and white, with no breathing being to witness it. But the dance around the earth of particles that I couldn't see assumed a stage thousands of miles away in the amber light of the moon, deepening umber and angry red. I awoke by chance at the moment of complete eclipse. He set the alarm twice, got up twice, peered through the bedroom window to see a gray shadow beginning to inch over white and hours later the same image in reverse, too early, too late.

Despite Her Pearls

I tapped my fingers on the card table and watched him checking the water, which refused to boil. His fine hair tumbled over his wire rims as he tipped the lid and peered into the pot. Brian shoved back the sleeves of his work shirt, revealing pale forearms and a scar like a fishhook near the elbow. He popped open the jar of Ragu and poured the lumpy contents, redolent of garlic and oregano, into a yellow pot chipped and rusted at the base where the flame licked insistently. I was allergic to garlic. With machismo he added a daub of oil to the water and emptied the carton of Ronzoni #2 into the pot. Spaghetti was his revenge, exacted with the finesse of a young man on his own. And I sat poised, like an artichoke.

As the pasta went limp, he stirred it with a metal fork and regulated the flame for a steady boil. The sauce began to spit. I sifted through his music collection, selected Cream, and looked out the window at the backs of brownstones on West 74th Street, one shouldering the next, their windows cloaked in makeshift curtains, tangled spider plants, and pull-down shades yellowed by sun and oily fingerprints. He dumped the pot of water into a colander, and the strands slipped over the rim in a rush like stocked fish poured into a new pool. Trapped by overhanging cabinets, the steam fogged his glasses, and he took them off just long enough to wipe them on his shirttails. One eye wandered without them, and he didn't want to look at me that way.

I stared at the carbohydrates ballooning sumptuously to the circumference of my plate. With a Swiss Army knife he uncorked a bottle of Mouton Cadet, and from a supermarket bag he pulled an Italian bread, soft as a baby's thigh. He stared at me. "Beats broccoli and plain yogurt." It wasn't even a rhetorical question. In my railroad apartment on East 83rd, he had eaten the flowers, abandoned the stalks, and attacked the logic of my subsistence. Now I hummed to

33

"Strange Brew" and poked at my pasta emerging here and there from the lumps of tomato. He twirled the long strands round and round his fork till the ends were fully engaged (the Italians say you can tell a man's character by the way he eats his spaghetti) and forwarded the album to "Sunshine of Your Love." What enticing tension.

Like pasta itself, we hailed from different worlds. The Chinese were making noodles back in 3000 B. C. The Arabs brought pasta to Sicily when they invaded in the 8th century. I was a Philadelphia WASP, he a French Canadian from Nashua, New Hampshire. The Chinese made starchy pasta from breadfruit, the Arabs used hard durum wheat.

The first time I met Brian's family, I wore a stiff white brace that ran from my collarbone to my lips. I had cracked a vertebra diving off his shoulders into seawater that was deceptively shallow. His father, Ed, was sitting in a beach chair outside the clapboard house, binoculars in one hand, Sam Adams in the other. He wore only a mesh baseball cap and faded gray shorts, his belly straining the top button. He greeted me with a kiss, Brian with a tweak to the cheek as he quipped—so how much do you weigh these days? When he and his wife heard about my accident, they nodded as if I were reporting on a trip to the supermarket—Cheerios, yes, two for one sale, no kidding. One of their fourteen cats slid across Ed's lap, and he raised his voice a few octaves to converse with it, the cat purring conspiratorially and arching its chocolate back. Inside, sunbeams lit red geraniums in the windowsills and rippled over boxes of Triscuits and Lucky Charms. Brian's mother had a pot of hamburger, onions, and tomato sauce, dubbed American chopped suey, huffing and bubbling on the stove, and she assumed you'd take some whenever you got hungry. She smiled benignly, pulled down the sleeves of her aqua sweatshirt, and returned to her recliner and the Red Sox.

The first time Brian met my family, he slept till 2 p.m. and (ambling dreamily into the kitchen) announced that he wasn't used to such clean sheets. My mother, dressed in gray slacks hemmed a little too short, shot a menacing look at my father, who concealed a slight smile as he resumed slathering mayonnaise on extra-thin white bread. By that hour the mahogany table had been oiled to a dull sheen and set for dinner at 7. My mother had ironed the diaphanous linens, polished the silver butter dish, set the dinner forks, salad forks, fish knives, dessert spoons, coffee spoons, and butter knives in their wonted positions. The rich soil smell of chrysanthemums and zinnias stole through the kitchen as she clipped the stems, trimmed the feathery leaves, and set each flower in a wire mesh at the bottom of a silver bowl. On the countertop were snippets of dill and a metal whisk coated with sour cream. The cold salmon would be ready at 4, giving her ample time to decorate it with a row of finely sliced cucumbers and a perimeter of lettuce, sliced tomatoes, and basil from her garden. Brian and my father sat in stuffed white chairs and talked bonds. I sat on the brick floor and stroked the silver hair of my Siberian husky. When I was eighteen, she had driven with me from Anchorage across the Rockies and farms of the Midwest to the muggy Main Line, sleeping under the car at night, her cavern beneath the muffler and transmission. My parents had had to add a foot of unsightly wire to the post and rail that encircled the property. To compensate, she graced the cool stones of the terrace wall, a svelte and dark-eyed wolf.

My family had a cabin, or *camp* as such retreats were called, in a preserve in the Pocono Mountains, originally a Quaker settlement when my grandfather built the place in the '20s, more recently a social club for upper-crust Philadelphians and New Yorkers. My extended family often gathered there in June, before the summer season raged with sailfish races and cocktail parties on red and white party boats that puttered across the man-made lake. As kids my brother and I climbed in the rafters that supported the roof and leapt on the beds, whose rusty springs jangled under our weight. Getting up in the dark before the grownups, we paddled a canoe through mist lifting off the lake and cast our hula poppers and listened to the line wheezing for a delicious moment, then the plop, and the wait. We rode around the lake on our bikes and on the tailgate of the Ford wagon, hurling rocks at mailboxes, breaking just about every stricture possible of our Main Line lives. During the slow June evenings the men disappeared to the trout stream, the women made potatoes and peas, waiting till the men lumbered back in their waders, smelling of hemlock and musk. As deftly as my father unhooked a trout and slipped it into his creel,

Brian eased into this culture, learning the rarified art of trout fishing, consuming the customary post-fishing gin and tonics, and replacing rotted boards on the front porch—we WASPs were rarely idle until the long dinners around the circular table my grandfather had built, anchored to a tree trunk that emerged from a hole in the floorboards.

"Let's clear," I nudged Brian's elbow one night.

"Sure," he got up and circled behind my mother, taking her plate first, then my father's. But instead of carrying them to the kitchen, he continued around, stacking one plate on top of the next, plates so thick you could hurl them at your mother-in-law and they wouldn't break.

"Brian," my mother called, crossing her arms over her Irish sweater, "that's not the way we do it in our house."

He stopped in his tracks like a coyote gauging a bear, turned on his heels and retreated to the kitchen where he scraped dishes and clattered pots at rock concert decibels.

Twice a year we made cursory visits to his house. In November the living room would be dark, a fire hissing from the wood-burning stove. Upstairs the bedroom doors were left open under the ill-proven assumption that sufficient heat would travel from the stove up the stairs and down the hallway and into six bedrooms. Ed never went to bed. Unlike my father, who donned his Brooks Brothers pajamas with white piping and drawstring and positioned his slippers by his bed, Ed flopped on this sofa or that and might well be on his ham radio at 3 a.m. He talked more to W1UXR and Q2BST than to us, a key topic being the reception from the forty-foot antenna he'd erected in the back yard. He ate cereal mixed with peanut butter out of a tumbler and any scraps on anyone's plate—this virtuoso trumpet player wasn't proud.

"Soooo," he'd warble, grinning at me. "Do you think you can put up with us?" He'd hurl that one at me semi-annually and I'd splutter, "But of course," wishing for some witticism on his frequency.

My mother irked my unflappable husband. His father made me queasy. I don't credit them with knowing that their jibes at our differences only threw us together. From unlikely roots came something new, like a hard slick egg. Our spaghetti war subsided. I grazed the supermarket aisles, tossing boxes of Ronzoni into the cart, caring little if it were pappardelle or farfalle, racchette or radiatore, egg or spinach, domestic or imported. Pasta became routine, as it did for the Italians post-Arab invasion.

By end of the week, the refrigerator shelves would be bare, revealing a film of stale milk, partial rings of raspberry jam, a sticky streak of grapefruit juice. From the vegetable drawers I pulled a half onion, two celery stalks, two thirds of a zucchini, a red pepper whose loosening skin creased slightly to the touch. In the back was a blue box with two mushrooms left. I ran the rubbery pieces under water, watching flecks of dirt spiral down the disposal, but they stayed brown and blotchy like hands on which age marks quite suddenly appear. When I tried to slice them, they dented and crumbled under the press of the knife. He wouldn't care, and if he did, he wouldn't complain. I stir-fried the vegetables, trying to catch the peppers before slaughtering all vitality, threw in some oregano and salt, and heaped the medley on top of linguini whose wide bands bore the weight with fortitude.

"Good veggies," he remarked, though their wholesomeness had seeped days ago into the vacuous air of the Whirlpool. "Garlic really makes the dish."

"Different from last week?"

"Oh, yeah."

We both knew neither of us could remember, and neither of us cared. Still, I made bow ties with withered broccoli, angel hair stuck tragically with jarred pesto, ziti with Kraft parmesan, all improvised, all greeted with acceptance if not tenderness. There is a pleasure in being creative when no one expects it and when the parameters of creativity are small. Years passed.

Frugality and fatigue landed us at a crossroads. Each had compromised, first to the other, then to our children. Faced with a plate of spaghetti, our daughter coated it with a blizzard of cheese, picked up single strands with her pudgy fingers, swirled the whole concoction around with her fork till red sauce shot over her mat by centrifugal force, feigned illness, and finally cried that spaghetti tasted like worms. Six years of makeshift baked ziti ensued. Brian endured.

At last he retaliated with recipes. Who could blame him? Now I bought the plum tomatoes and heavy cream, chopped the shallots, set out the measuring cup, and he donned the apron. He discovered fresh pasta. He embarked on fettucini with fervor, stirring cream and butter and cheese with a wire whisk and watching the gentle roll of bubbles around the noodles, setting the timer for total precision, and tossing the mixture gently with two wooden spoons. When he made it, the conglomerate cohered. When I tried, pale puddles of cream and discrete chunks of cheese lay abandoned in the pan.

As the children grew up and moved on, his sights were set on ever finer wines like those he drank with my father, while mine were aimed at identifying the necessary ingredients of my American chopped suey. The tenor of a marriage is never what anyone else predicts. I stand under the perpetual light of the supermarket (and think of Alaska) and press my thumb against the skin of a honeydew, divining some give where the stem was severed, cupping in my palms a silky green cusp rimmed with white seeds and feeling the juice slide down my throat, just sweet enough, but I won't know till I pay $1.99 and lug it home and take a knife to it.

My father used to offer my mother a puckered peck on the cheek now and then, and they didn't hug in my presence. Nor did I ever hear him argue with her, politics excepted. Now I wonder if silence doesn't have some advantages. If you complain about the baby blue spittle in the sink or the boxers on the floor, you send tremors underground whose potential only the most sensitive seismograph can calibrate.

"So does it really matter?"

"Not really."

"Then why bring it up?"

"I haven't said a critical word in five years."

"You have no sense of time."

"I don't want to *look* at your underwear…"

"Then look the other way. Do you think I expect you to pick them up?"

"Seems plausible."

"Don't take boxers personally. "

"They're pretty personal."

And very quickly you've taken on sexism, aesthetics, moral imperative, and concepts of time and space. Admittedly, he can't win. If he's defensive, he's stereotypically male. If he repairs the situation, which he invariably does, I feel guilty for being his mother, or rather my mother.

Silence with the self-restraint of courtship is one thing, lassitude another. The ease of custom, the inch of fat around the waist and in the bank, the hush where children once cried when nightmares threw hulking figures against the blinds afford all too much space for the kind of love that myths of marriage promise. Between the morning and evening commute pass twenty years at war and at sea. Seven p.m. finds me, paring knife in hand, wondering who this man is who bursts through the door in his navy overcoat and Italian hat, who drops the briefcase stuffed with *Fortune* and the *Times*, who asks me matter-of-factly about my day. And what did he think when he descended the steps of the subway at Times Square or rose to his office on the 42nd floor or interviewed a young writer from Barnard? Shall I tell him that the new sofa looks like something my great Aunt Lucy might own, that our eighteen-year-old daughter is utterly in love as she won't be again (he'll deny it), that my mother is losing her caustic edge and I miss it (he won't believe it), that while I ask I may not always hear? What is revealed depends on who writes the epic, and usually no one does.

"I don't feel like cooking tonight."

"Let's just have pasta."

"I have some ravioli—red pepper for you, cheese—"

"Fine, go light on the parm. Cholesterol—"

"I know."

Boiling water is like getting married. It's easy. You just turn on the flame and wait a few minutes without looking too closely. But turning durum wheat into something edible is hard, or used to be. Early Sicilians kneaded the dough for an entire day, stomping on it with bare feet as the Mediterranean sun arose, gathered heat like a branding iron, lingered at its zenith with glaring clarity, and finally relented, allowing the return of shade.

Americans eat pasta 2.7 times per week and have sex 2.1 times per week. They consume 24 pounds of pasta per capita annually. Pasta consumption has risen since the '60s because it's no longer considered fodder for the working class. Marriage has been declining since the '70s. About half of American marriages end in divorce. Average duration is eight years. Mass production makes smooth pastas from which sauces slip like raw egg. Average cooking time is 10-12 minutes. My friend tells me that when she has sex with her husband she thinks about something else. "Don't you feel lonely?" I ask. She laughs, "For about 10 minutes."

A myth still circulates that on his travels Marco Polo brought pasta from China to Venice. Other stories hint it was an Italian sailor who learned the cuisine from his Chinese mistress.

At the beginning of a marriage you live the myths without recognizing them as such. Later you choose. If the world I came from ever had any cachet, I'm sure the allure has dwindled. And if his world was refreshingly unassuming, by now it's banal. So what is the bequest to our children? I find my son reading our family history, which records the first ancestor who arrived here as an indentured servant in 1638, eloped with the daughter of the landowner, lived in a cave, was finally reconciled with the family and established in a mansion of his own. My son framed my father's Bronze Star Medal to hang on his wall and painstakingly glued together the shattered pieces of an urn that the Blackfeet gave my grandfather when he did legal work for them in the early 1900s. My daughter reports that her college friends often gibe at her WASPiness, she with the rosy cheeks and fine hair, a bent for tennis and grilled fish. Others, struck by her propriety, consider her French, and she glows, privately unsure what to make of the Canadian part and willing to let it slide. Her friends see all this more clearly than I.

My son has reached the age at which I first met my husband. He takes his girlfriend to restaurants where they order a decent Bordeaux, eat organic greens, aged sirloin, and warm chocolate mousse cake in a swirl of raspberry, and he picks up the tab despite her pearls.

Our 25th anniversary arrived like a FedEx package with no return address. There it was at our doorstep on an otherwise nondescript Tuesday. I sat at the kitchen table and wondered what to make for dinner, wondered what was the composition of 25 years. I searched the cabinets rather than the cookbooks. Among the boxes of Grape Nuts and tins of English Breakfast tea, I found a jar of artichoke pesto, a can of tomato paste, and three open packages of fettucini.

His mother sent a Hallmark card with purple violets and a rhyme. My mother called the next day full of apologies. She couldn't imagine how she had forgotten. Did we go to Le Bernardin? Did we order champagne? Did he give me silver? No, Mom. Blue beads. Chianti. Spaghetti. You're kidding. Nope. It was good.

One night about eight months later, I happened to remark, "This dinner is just like the one on our anniversary."

"Didn't we go out?"

"We had spaghetti."

"Really?"

As my fork twirled the fettucini winding languorously under mushrooms and plum tomatoes, I smiled at the blossoming of possibility. What now would be my weapon of revenge?

Monday Moments

Yesterday, today, and tomorrow 42,000 gallons of oil seeped, seep, and will seep into the Gulf of Mexico. I open my refrigerator and heft a gallon of milk, spilling some as I tip it on the lip of a glass.

My mother lies on her back in her hospital bed, nearly sleeping, while NBC news rattles on about volcanic ash. She can't turn it off and the nurse is down the hall eating take-out Chinese.

A restraining order is out on Ricky, the drummer in my husband's band. (Ricky has diabetes and no job, and his twin, Vince, is dying of the same disease. They usually stay home all day and play video games. Age: 44.) Ricky found out his mom has been cashing his disability checks for the last two years, so he threw an ashtray at her and drew a knife, she called the cops, and he spent a night in jail. Now he's out on East 11th in the rain under the eave of his building. Now he has his insulin because he snuck back in to get it. My husband is faintly amused. Quite a story for folks in Westchester. "This is the guy you play music with every week?" (Chuka chukka beats the ice in the silver walls of his martini maker.) "And everyone in the band lives in the city?" He answers as if I don't already know.

I miss a call from my friend Olivia, an art conservator in Manhattan who went to all the right schools (Milton, Brown, etc.), just got laid off and doesn't know how she's going to put her twins through college. It's staggering, 100 K a year. She wasn't raised to niggle; it isn't in her blood, Olivia of the sparkling inflection and pearls.

I see Tanya behind leaded Tudor windows around the corner from my house in the gloaming of her 72 inch TV. Her husband cheated for ten years and she just found out. When her friends bike with him, she feels they have betrayed her and spends hours composing emails to them. I know because she sends me another draft.

CNN booms: Afghan girls were gassed at school today. "We're going tomorrow," they say. "We will not stop." Last year a girl at the school where I teach missed 40 days. She visited a lot of colleges. Consequently, we have a rule: you can't miss more than 20% of classes in a particular subject without risk of failure of that course.

The fridge exhales cool air while I pour. Mashed potatoes lie pocked and congealed in a tinfoil takeout container. How Annie used to love them, the cold ones, Annie, who used to live at my house because her dad never got out of his pajamas and her mom was on barbiturates *and* alcohol so my mom took her to appointments and fed her things other than Fritos and Coke.

At this moment a guy barges through the outside door of my daughter's pre-war building in Soho and breaks into the apartment directly below hers. She is alone on the queen mattress reading *Moby-Dick*. Of course I find this out later so perhaps it doesn't count. Only the mattress and *Moby-Dick* count. And Prada perfume wafting from her cardigan on the floor.

At this moment Southeast Asia is sleeping. I don't need to say I am not.

At this moment milk is leaving the carton and filling my blue glass, blue as the Indian Ocean at noon and only slightly darker above the limit of milk.

At this moment wind hurtles confetti off the apple tree onto the sidewalk, a bustle arises among the oak leaves, and yellow dust like the dust of moth wings invisible in the night air settles on my jacket left in the grass where I will see it tomorrow and brush it away without a thought for the flourishes of breathtaking wind that will have died.

I think of Matthew to whom I wrote a poem at age fourteen and, yes, after hearing him play Chopin, slipped it into his pocket. An Italian woman married him and divorced him and set herself up in a West Village apartment to paint. When I saw him a month ago, he hugged me with boyish relish, and I smelled oxford shirts oiled at the neck and houses with all the blinds down and cigarettes—the smell of my uncle who dragged his feet and came for every Thanksgiving.

They're burning the oil on the surface of the Gulf while 5000 feet deep the rig vomits 29 gallons in any given minute, in every minute.

I put on Bach to order the dissonance in each instant. The melody travels from bass clef to treble like a continuous strip of silk. The bass ripples a repeated open E flat chord to stabilize the melody. I can't find mathematical relations between martinis and insulin, between love and betrayal, between freedom and entitlement, between infatuation and disintegration, between the intruder and the innocent. I ride on the hilly notes for a moment. We give ourselves breaks.

I arrange some daisies in an old jar, wipe bits of parmesan and toast off the counter. At 30 you always want to be in the presence of the other; at 50 you think every minute about what the other is doing and with whom. The first is love, the second jealousy. The first is ethereal, the second visceral. The first shines merrily because it sees no end, the second burns with the voltage of blue fire because it revels in hell.

Women are jealous, men fearful. Jealousy is stronger than love though love is the premise for jealousy. It bleeds like drops of ink in water. It draws back the curtain on an empty stage where a voice whittles words over and over and over in the brittle space that is 4 a.m., a time of utterly distorted clarity.

There is Tristan on his deathbed, his deathbed! And even then Isolde #2, his wife, lies to him. "The sails are black, Tristan," she cries. And if they are black, Isolde #1, his love, is not aboard en route to his aid. He dies of grief, she dies of grief. A rose tree grows from her grave, a vine from his that embraces the tree and sprouts anew each time it is cut. Love defies death, but jealousy defied love.

Who thinks of such things? It's Monday. Just Monday in suburban USA, and the anomalous Bach sonatas have reached a dramatic diminuendo. School buses grind down the hill. My neighbor's dog yaps at a chipmunk. My neighbor curses out his girlfriend, whose monochromatic cries through the screen door are as unintelligible as cotton wool.

It's true that my son's first word was *saaa*, and his best friend's was *shu.* He pronounced it explosively, she murmured it insistently. At eleven months she was blue eyed and quick, he brown eyed and methodical. Their first words were a kind of coupling, one of purpose, necessity, and comfort. They used to climb into her crib, she scaling the bars more nimbly than he, and sit facing each other as they pulled off their socks. His were white with mealy gray soles, and he pulled them halfway up his stocky calves. Hers slumped around her ankles making little tires of orange and purple and red, one mismatched with the other. *saaa* and *shu*. I do, I do. Yet she married a woman, and he married another.

II

Fin

I

At 11 a.m. on New Year's Eve my dog stares at me, square in the eyes, from under a brow of black curls as if he wants to know. He wears a translucent lampshade on his head to keep him from gnawing the stitches in his left leg where a mast cell tumor was removed six days before. During the night Fin scratched so hard he pulled off the collar and his ferocious licking of the wound woke my husband. He looks sheepish and slightly absurd, those perpetually gentle eyes with cusps along the bottom rim, milky and red, as he looks up. The area above his hock is spongy, the stitches bristling, the incision bright like coils on an electric stove. He itches all over, a stealthy legacy of the tumor, said the vet, and I give him Benadryl pills wrapped in bologna. After scratching to go out, he stands under the pine tree staring blankly, severed from his olfactory reality by a good ten inches. He scrounges through the ferns like a blind man in a supermarket. At night I hear his leg drumming against plastic in a fruitless attack. I hear plastic whapping into coffee tables and chairs and brushing and thumping the carpet on the stairs as the rim of the collar catches. Last night he barked at one, three, and four a.m., a piercing bark that swerved into my consciousness like a driver out of control. I tottered down the stairs and slumped at the kitchen table, blinking my sticky eyes, while he hustled outside. Through the black windows I couldn't discern his black form at all, only the ghostly lampshade moving back and forth across the yard.

At noon we are back at the vet's. I sit on the edge of a bench in the miniscule waiting room, and Finny quivers and leans into my knees while the vet's pug scuttles around breathing heavily and two parrots in a cage to my left vituperate like caustic tenants at a coop meeting.

49

It's a small-town family operation, the large vet in jeans and his large wife in a long flowy skirt with crinkly gray hippie hair down to her waist. With her hearty arms, each bearing at least a dozen tin brace-lets, she lifts Finny onto the table. Somehow the incision burst open and wet flesh like a persimmon glistens under fluorescent light. Fuck, says the vet. You'll have to leave him here for a few hours. His Santa Claus eyes squint from his thick unshaven cheeks. The malignant cells started as immune cells to combat an allergy, he says. Now they've shifted allegiance and traveled to the perimeter of the battleground, possibly launching into the great unknown like pioneers looking for waterways to the west. Yet it's not romantic. The vet prescribes tran-quilizers and antibiotics and recommends we start chemotherapy at the end of the week. Since the treatment is systemic, I decide against the blood test that would reveal if the cancer has spread.

2:00 on New Year's Eve: the woodsy smell of coffee is seeping up the stairs. My son sits at the table reading about the bombing of Syria and eating a banana muffin. Later he'll go into Manhattan to cele-brate with his friends who graduated from college last spring and have no idea what to do with their lives. They get odd jobs from Craig's list, take kids on wilderness trips, wait tables at diners, enter training programs at investment firms, and gravitate toward graduate school where careers remain categories rather than realities.

Upstairs I dump the laundry on his bed, and Paul comes up to sort and fold, separating his clothes from ours, and stuffing them into a duffel. I glance at the oak desk, the college diploma leaning against the wall, the rows of art books propped between stereo speakers, the shelves of LPs—my old Beatles albums, Cream, Doors, Temptations. On his desk is a leather pad and pen set that sat on his grandfather's desk in his law office in Philadelphia. Every day my father would snatch his briefcase, slam the screen door, and drive to his office in his seersucker or tweeds in a quixotic foreign car. At 80 he was diagnosed with lung cancer, which traveled to his once acute brain and killed him three months later.

By 4:00 my husband has brought Finny home, and he lies at my feet. "Fin, ah Feeee-un," I say, stroking his flank. Lately he senses a new poignancy in my touch and capitalizes on it, leaning against my knees in a near swoon. But now, basking in a Jacuzzi of refracted light and still drugged, he doesn't budge. The light reveals my fingerprints on his collar, flecks of dirt, and dried streams where water dribbled from his chin. But he's only six.

He's the baby, the third child, the spoiled one. More spousal fights have erupted over him than over the kids. With the latter, my husband always deferred: "Go ask your mother, she knows the rules." Whereupon he would resume reading the *Times* and complete the crossword. But Fin, he knew a soft touch. Feigning sleep at my husband's end of the table, he'd get up from time to time to check the progress on Brian's plate, black nostrils just quivering over the table rim. A scrap of pork left, a roll. A little more time. Brian would look at him, crooning, yes, I have something for you at which point Fin's tail would get going and low whines begin to roll from his throat ballooning into shrill outright demands just as I snap, "Don't look at him, don't even look his way!"

"Who me, what'd I do?"

Despite scientific evidence to the contrary, Brian was of the opinion Fin's diet was inadequate without table food. This was a matter of sheer empathy, an admirable trait in a spouse, but Fin was on the receiving end of most of it especially when a doctor suggested Brian slow his intake of triple crème brie, the beginning of the end; soon he'd be eating dry kibble twice a day and life would not be worth living.

I rummage in a cabinet for an extra frying pan for Paul, who's moving out. I never moved back after college, after all. God no. But my parents were *old*, I reason, and about as spontaneous as Kant or chicken soup. In Paul's twenty-two years of life I should have realized he'd do something "for good," and he'd be gone. But child rearing, from the point of view of the novice parent, is a morass of transitions—teething, talking, tooth fairies and blasted myths of tooth fairies, confirmations and graduations, lies and rebellion, new sneakers, pimples, ingrown toenails, broken wrists, pot. It's not about ends because, like homework, there's always more.

Or like dog walks. So far we've clocked 6,570 circuits around the neighborhood, reversing direction every week or so for new views on life.

Or the ripple effect. Fin chewed a corner of linoleum which meant replacing the whole floor, at which point sanding the existing wood seemed brilliant, but once that was done the other floors looked like shit, so we vacated not to die of polyurethane fumes, resulting in a few hundred dropped at a nearby inn that wouldn't take dogs, so we paid for him at a precious kennel that doesn't crate the dogs. Boom: $2360.

Once long ago there was the eternity of babyhood. My daughter, brimming with nurturing hormones at age eleven, carried her puppy in her arms upstairs and down, lifted him when a garbage truck growled too close and he froze in his little tracks, balking at her tug on the red leash. He brought out her most patient self witnessed to date when he gnawed through her fifth pair of flip-flops, the thick ones, ate her cell phone, stole cookies right out of her hand, shredded her homework of course—ate my students' homework too—and still she carried him about, his ever larger paws draped over her shoulder, his ears cocked as if posing for *Puppy Vogue*. "I bonded with him in his infancy," she would later say.

While "sivilized" children were at school, Fin was out back, forelegs scrambling rapid fire as he dug up daffodil bulbs and left their brittle skins among the daisies and crabgrass; he rolled in grass seed, leaving craters of naked dirt; he scaled chicken wire and dug under a post and rail, ate a rope hammock, butter off the counter. And there was the case of the missing spoons.

Further mystery. "To my dying day," puzzles my husband, martini in hand, peering over my shoulder while I sauté shallots, "never will I understand why Fin leaves the room while his supper is being prepared." It's true. At the clank of the kibble jar, he leaves the kitchen, lies in the hall, and wanders in nonchalantly once a cup of Eukanuba is dumped in a dish. Fin is a class act.

Paul, also, waits till the food is ready, but for different reasons. Sometimes at dinner he pushes back his chair and lifts Fin onto his lap, this big sprawling dog with his back legs spread open, front ones flopping. For a moment he rests his head on Paul's shoulder, then scrambles, ill at ease. Paul doesn't have the paternal touch yet, which is just as well. He's on the move, and Fin knows. He plops down and resumes his position by Brian's chair, an opportunist who spreads his affection around the family, more politic than our previous dog, or Huey Long.

I try to exploit Brian's newfound interest in psychology. "So why is our son dating *that* girl?"

"Beats me. I wouldn't."

There I am eyes wide open at night tracing a zigzag crack in the ceiling and wondering how that girl and I are different and how I'll deal with her at Christmas and Thanksgiving. I'm not as politic as Fin.

The family configuration will change. I accept that in the abstract and convince myself I'm halfway there.

Around 7 p.m. Finny heaves himself up and sways to the top of the stairs. His front paws extend in front of him, and he dips his head in a futile attempt to lick the shaved area where the vet inserted needles during surgery. Poised like a sphinx, he stares down the stairs toward the front door, his eyes half hidden under a curtain of black curls, his white chest bright like a dress shirt, anticipating something—it's New Year's Eve after all—and we're all balanced on the fulcrum between what we've done and what we will do.

I look back, Brian ahead. At the moment he's staring into the screen of his laptop, as if into a crystal ball, reading about tumors. His eyes water and he claims he forgot his allergy pills. We don't know everything yet, I say, irritated. He gets up, leans against the counter, crosses his arms, visibly swallowing his thoughts. I shouldn't shut him down. Twenty-first century men are supposed to show their emotions, and I'm usually trying to draw him out and enrich the spaghetti dinners during commercial breaks from Anderson Cooper. How do you feel about your mom's Parkinson's, how do you feel about your boss?

"It is what it is," he shrugs, eyeing my plate because I never eat the last bite and he knows who will.

It's New Year's Eve and there will be steak scraps for Fin—fat pure and simple—unencumbered by the weight of time and assessment of accomplishments to date. Still, the extra notch of pity for his suffering is in the air, and Fin's going to exploit it, as human males do with head colds.

Finny also looks ahead. Out for the evening walk, he anticipates the biscuit to be had on return. Once a certain corner is turned, he's charging with the zeal of customers at Walmart on Black Friday. He has honed his survival skills here in the affluent suburbs of Westchester, something we should all do just in case.

By 10 Paul is in the city sauntering along some avenue, hands in his jeans pocket, his grandfather's black overcoat offering partial shelter against the wind and light snow sparkling in the streetlights, drifting from party to party with people I don't know, people I'll never know. They listen to Jay Z and Rick Ross and Lil Wayne. I mean, DMX is practically a neighbor with his stone house behind bars up in Bedford. One of us. So I guess Paul will be back.

"How do you feel about him leaving?" I ask, eyeing the contingent from South Dakota getting pumped on TV. A long wait in ten-degree weather for a metal ball to fall.

"It's what he should do."

"Of course."

At 11 the phone rings and I dart into Paul's room to answer it. A scattering of change and a note from someone I don't know lie on the bureau, and a scent of Old Spice snaps me into his presence as surely as the smell of certain molasses cookies reignites my childhood. It's my brother in Wisconsin who wishes me happy New Year, prematurely, and tells me he has prostate cancer, the most aggressive kind. If it hasn't spread, they can do radiation; if it has, there isn't anything they can do except, says the doctor, pray, the tacit understanding between me and my brother being, no one's doing that. "Pretty weird," he says, "Here I am *wishing* I just have prostate cancer." Pacing with my phone, eyes blurring like snow outside a dark window, I nearly trip over Finny. How could I miss him with his lampshade collar? He has rolled on his back in anticipation of a belly rub and eyes me with near disdain. You can't deny me. And he knows I won't. Silence on the line. I don't know what to say. My brother. Except I can't believe it. Survive. Don't be anxious about what hasn't happened yet. I squat

54

and rub the slope of Fin's belly from the smudgy white chest to the thinning hair near his groin.

The confluence of events is fictive. Who would believe it?

I can't.

New Year's Eve is long. What's quick is the flick of the red clock at midnight, then a hiccup in time before we ask—where are we now?

On TV crowds are dispersing from Times Square, and a blizzard of tickertape lies underfoot. White blood cells and red, bone cells and marrow, obedient cells and cells in riot are preparing to divide.

II

Labor Day. Fin has dug a nice cool hole in the dirt against the wall at the back of our property. He peers at me from behind the trunk of a pine that has lost its lower branches. He watches my every move now, following me when I go inside, standing at the low window and staring out when I get in my car. He's old. But I don't know what he needs now that he didn't before.

The texture of his hair has changed. It's lighter, less curly, less black though not gray. I try Black Pearl Shampoo and Conditioner, but like Shiseido wrinkle cream, it doesn't have lasting effect. Mulch from the yard and leaves that fell early because of a draught cling to his coat and litter the house when he comes inside.

It's been five days since the last surgery, and the lampshade lies in the corner of the kitchen. The vet said we wouldn't need it at all this time, that Fin was so old and stiff he probably couldn't reach the stitches near his anus where another tumor was removed. But as soon as the anesthesia wore off, he was at it, curled in a ball, gnawing at the stitches and licking with all his healing power focused in the muscles of his tongue. A fifty-pound dog with a homespun haircut, survivor of four surgeries and a month of chemo.

By now the itching has subsided and we free him from his collar. The tumor came from male hormones, the vet said, and he'd probably get another unless we neutered him. (Baldness results from male hormones too, according to my husband, but he has not taken desperate measures.) I've never seen the point of circumcision or any of that meddling, but I have little expertise in the matter, being female and interior and deriving femaleness from factors other than the overtly sexual. "Once he's out," laughed the assistant vet who had no idea of Fin's heroic victories over cancer, "of course we should neuter him."

Of course? Fin tiptoes around miniature poodles. He assumes the submissive position when a terrier merely clears his throat, just as my father opted to remain silent when my mother yapped about dirty socks left on the floor, or his inability to fix a leaky faucet, or his third bourbon, which she considered excessive. "I wanted him to fight back," she later confided, "to be strong." My father probably thought there was manliness in restraint, but he wouldn't have articulated that.

Fin's true love was a stalwart male boxer that snarled and charged when we approached. While I cringed, Finny pranced. He'd smell the dog a hundred yards away and dash into the woods while I sprinted behind, yelling futile commands until I found him whining and dancing around the boxer whose owner waited patiently, her dog on a leash, while I attempted to catch mine. Fin had spark, not swagger. And like an aristocrat of ancient Greece, he didn't split hairs about sexual orientation.

When I took Fin for stitches removal, I said, "The dog has lost his drive. He lies around all day."

Again the upstart assistant laughed, "It takes a few weeks for the hormones to get out of the system, it's not that."

It's definitely *that*. Months later Fin has further refined the art of immobility to an even greater extent than my father who, while still in possession of his jewels, found running depressing and considered diving into a pool and gliding to the other end sufficient exercise for the day. As the sun rages and temperatures accelerate to three digits, Fin lies on his side on the cool stone hallway and fails to respond when I put on the leash and tug, pulling him across the floor.

Once I nudge him with my foot and he realizes the inevitable (like the third alarm after you hit snooze three times) he's up. Outside, a scent in his elaborate olfactory world captivates us and we linger while he snuffs and grunts and paws at an old clump of leaves to get closer to a trace of deer, another dog, a bit of pizza crust spilled from a garbage can, at which point I try to enumerate three external stimuli that lit my world today and decide if they're more or less ephemeral than pizza crust.

At noon the sun has topped the old oaks and maples leaning over the backyard, and sunlight blares with the relentless intensity of oil trucks grinding up the hill. These are siesta hours for Fin. No meals going on right now, his primary *raison d'etre* like most men over the age of twenty-five.

All over the country men are flicking on their electric grills, pouring kerosene on nuggets of charcoal, flipping burgers, marinating steaks, swigging beer, munching chips. Even the oak leaves are heavy, sagging in the humidity and scarcely quivering when a breeze happens to pass. Hemlock limbs and the furling backs of maple leaves are as weathered and dull as Fin's coat or my mother's hands.

Half my family looks ahead to fall evenings that nip your cheeks when you step outside after work and it's already dark, the other half looks back to the lassitude of summer shorts and blue hydrangea nodding in clusters over the back fence. It's immaterial; we have to resume our drive and accelerate into real or imagined productivity, Fin excepted. There he lies in the dirt, deaf to my calls, deaf to the school buses grinding up the hill with a new cargo of kids off to meet new legions of teachers. He has retired from the long walks up and down hills overlooking the Hudson. The circumference of his world is shrinking, like my mother's.

Last night she went to the hospital again. She doesn't swallow well, and some bit of bread or the tip of a bean lodged in her lungs like a fly on flypaper whose waxy wings vibrate uselessly as in a dream where the will cannot will one's feet to move. And so the lovely bit of white bread caused vomiting and a fever of 104. Years ago, when my mother's mind was as sharp as an eagle's beak, she signed a Living Will saying she didn't want feeding tubes and resuscitators; more recently her doctor discouraged other undue intervention that would be stressful for a woman her age. An aide called yesterday, needing permission to send my mother beyond the walls of the nursing home to save her life.

I wouldn't have let the vet give chemo to Fin if it did to dogs what it does to humans. At some point one suffers enough. And a dog suffers without knowing why, which makes it worse, some humans think, though a dog doesn't need to contemplate the odds of survival. Still, every day I would've looked at him and thought, I could be god and decide you should live longer, or try. The first time my mother was in the hospital with pneumonia, a doctor called to ask me about ventilators. I was driving to work, speeding along a suburban street where little kids waited for the bus. I didn't know about the Living Will or if I did I couldn't think of it *then*. Should I say yes to breathing? Cop lights flashed in my rearview mirror and veered past. I pulled off the road, my chest constricted, head on the steering wheel. "Yes." But then I came home and dug a yellowed document from the file cabinet and called him back.

Even so, she survived.

6 p.m. on Labor Day. The grill is hissing with fatty burgers, highways clogged with people heading home on the cusp of summer. I call my mother and tell her every bit of news I can think of because she doesn't say a word unless I say, Are you still there? And then she says, I'm here, so I talk about the US Open and Paul's new girlfriend and my new students and the tornado sweeping through the county, and even now the sun glints beneath an eggplant cloud and thunder growls far away beyond the strain of traffic on our hill, but then she falls asleep on the phone, and I sit on the back step staring at a little black screen with its connection to nothing, trying to think it's good that she sleeps, though I didn't say good-bye or I'll call you tomorrow.

And there is my son, the one who left forever but here he is, home for the weekend. Paul finds Fin's sheepskin toy lying in the dirt under a rhododendron, its stuffing and squeaker long disinterred. He waves it, and Fin prances, lifting his front paws, taking the toy and shaking it in his mouth as if it were a mouse he had to kill, but we know he has no killer instinct (especially now), and he drops the limp old thing—Paul throws it again, and Fin stares blankly around the yard till we point him in the right direction. Then he races to retrieve it and tears toward the fence, pulls a u-turn, dodges the rhododendrons and streaks across the tiny yard to the opposite side where he drops the toy and madly digs in the dirt, stops suddenly to see if we're watching, at which point Paul seizes the toy and tosses it as he did when he was five for Fin's predecessor, and I realize life recurs in parallel scenes more than we ever expect it to. Fin abandons his hole to race again around the yard, Paul lurching at him in a pretense of a tackle, which he would never do now since he's four times Fin's weight. My son left home an artist and returned a lawyer. In five minutes Fin returns to his cool spot by the back wall, panting. Paul oversees the steaks.

He used to be fast, really fast. Once Fin found a deer leg in the woods and I chased him for an hour before herding him towards the car, into which he leapt just to get a biscuit, maggoty deer leg in tow. When my mother was here for Christmas one year with her anxiety-ridden Westie, I spilled red wine on the rug, and we sprinkled some lethal white chemical stain remover on it, which the terrier ate. "Ye Gods," shrieked my white-haired mother, calling 911. My daughter held the dog in the sink, pouring cup after cup of water in her mouth while we hovered around in solicitous horror, and Fin tiptoed toward the table, grabbed the entire Christmas duck and fled.

He suffered no moral qualms. When his namesake stole a chicken now and then, he said his pap called it borrowing if you intended to pay it back. I didn't want the duck back. And Fin's rationale was a bit different: to him it was all in the family, and table food was his food, eventually. As Brian hurled himself at Fin with his trophy, I looked at him and shrugged: any woman blames her husband before her kids.

By 7:00 the oak branches are swirling and gray rain coats the windows on the river side of the house. I go up to get a long-sleeve shirt but stay in my shorts and flip-flops. As I push aside my summer dresses I look down and there is Fin. He has found me, and I give him a quick pat on the head. He looks up from under his black curls and one eye is filmy blue like the windowpanes right now, and white pus lines the lower rim. With one pat he is reassured of whatever it is he needs now and didn't need before. His needs are so easily met, and I wonder if my kids will have to wonder what I need to feel whole when I reach his age, which is 91 if we trust the human/dog ratio or 94 like my mother who quietly endures now spooning pureed food and dozing through time without the demarcations of a New Year or a Labor Day, joints in time that assemble past, present, and future into something nearly, but not quite, tangible.

Out the window I see the birch has already lost so many leaves, they lie around the trifurcated trunk like paper tears. One trunk stands half the height of the others, amputated in a freak snowstorm one year when the leaves were still on the trees and snow weighted the limbs till they snapped like chicken bones. Because fall is coming we'll hustle to the train tomorrow with renewed vigor. Because my mother is ever so slowly dying, I'll call tomorrow and wake her up. We sit down to eat as lightning flares through the house, lighting for an instant the green glasses filled with water, the swelling butter, the burnished kernels of corn, the fat veined steak. Fin takes his position at Brian's side, pants for a few minutes then falls asleep, certain of certain scraps.

To Arrest the Phases of the Moon

At night a leopard slipped onto the dirt road and turned ninety degrees without a backward glance. You could see his weight in the slowly rotating shoulder bone and huge paws; he was long from the low slung jaw to the tail like the S curve on a violin, and he marked his territory at calculated intervals. Driving the Van Wyck from JFK past low-rise apartments and Giants Stadium, I close my eyes to let the leopard pass and re-pass on the screen behind my eyelids, knowing he will turn off soon and go where we cannot follow.

I live fifteen minutes from the Bronx Zoo. I flew 9000 miles to see leopards and elephants living as if humans did not need to protect them from humans. Driving from the single airstrip to our bungalow, I saw a baby elephant nudging its mother as she emerged from a cluster of trees, and I had to text my daughter back home though my husband scoffed. Gradually other gray backs, tusks, and swishing tails appeared, eight-ton bodies with straight lumbering legs without visible knee joints. I heard their ears flap like a sail luffing, the suck and sigh of mud, water whoosh from trunks, dry grass bristle, bushes snap. I watched a male, weathered as old shingles, rest his trunk on his tusk and scratch his belly with his penis that touched the ground. Within hours I felt *nothing* was occurring in the world except this commonplace bathing in mud and consumption of leaves. It was entirely new.

But I learned the word *elephant* at two and wrote poems about elephants at eight, happily finding the word *lummox* and believing I'd captured the essence of elephantness. Through the plight of Babar, I could not but believe in the power of human generosity and the ease with which wild things adapt to us humans, Babar standing in a salon in green suit and spats, Babar puttering through the countryside in his

61

little red convertible. When I read the story to my own kids, I quickly flipped past the page where the hunter kills Babar's mother because, protective as that mother elephant in Africa, or any boomer parent, I didn't want my kids to entertain any notions of orphan-hood. All too real. And given the life expectancy of an affluent American female, that was scarcely a reality. What was inarguable, though distant, was the demise of sub-Saharan elephants, which were hunted by safaris for a half-century on reserves that until the 1960s protected them not as elephants, but as targets. Now the human obsession has turned from ivory to rhino horn, considered an aphrodisiac in China, and selling on the black market for $10,000 a pound. Such demand does not wait for an animal to die a natural death. Kill, hack, and leave otherwise intact a body that seems to have walked out of the pages of prehistory where it hobnobbed with stegosauruses and saber-toothed cats.

For hours we stared out at the bush, across fields and drying water holes, trying to spot life in the dead grass, behind shrubs, amongst leaves, easily missing an eagle perched on the limb of a leadwood, whose hard wood kept it standing long after the tree had died. These trees were common and easy to anthropomorphize with their gnarled limbs and arthritic fingers, these unburied dead who could not cross the Styx but stayed, alienated from a landscape of eating and mating. When not seeing animals, we saw evidence of them—termite hills, sticky wallows printed by elephant feet the size of dinner plates, and lumps of dung with undigested grass on its way to sinking back in the sandy dirt. It was elephant dung that rocked New York in 1999 when artist Chris Ofili used it to decorate the exposed breast of his black Madonna. That dung was not feces but *elephant*, essential metonymy, for a creature with a huge memory and an original nose, an animal that spreads her beautiful ears to appear even bigger than her mega-ton self, as the mother did when we approached. She had a baby, after all.

The hours of straining to see and absorb blurred like newsprint left out in the rain, leaving discrete words. Weeping wattle, white-tailed mongoose, lilac-breasted roller, croaking cisticola, kudu, nyala, steenbok, sneezewood, magic guarri, common false-thorn, jackal and klipspringer. The names had their own tempo, and denotation was enough. Sound seemed to bring me closer to sight.

One night our flashlight lit on a ribcage, open like symmetrical wings, inside the spiny branches of an acacia. The only flesh left was the liver, liquid red as though adrenaline still ran through it as the impala veered and leapt. One figure stood over the body, pausing—thick neck in profile, ears tipped back—as if he wanted to stretch out and sleep like a dog in the dust on a sultry afternoon. But soon the scent of blood would travel downwind and other hyenas would arrive. So he yanked the neck, antlers rose, and a triangular head turned as if to watch the jaw pop out the eye that had not been alert enough. He effaced hair and skin on the muzzle, teeth grating and cracking bone. Grind and crack splintered the backdrop of chirring crickets and a grey lourie's down-sliding call.

Behind the acacia a leopard lay in the grass. With her paws stretched out, she blinked drowsily as her cub strayed from sight and the hyena ate. Why so nonchalant? The impala was *her* kill. She had stalked low to the ground, waited, crept forward, gauged her position, shot out full length, leapt on the chest, clung as the impala careened, caught the neck and punctured the windpipe. It wasn't *fair* came an internal voice like that of a kid on a playground. Did she have a right because she had a child to feed, or was she just more beautiful and therefore more worthy? No question, I preferred tawny eyes, big paws and silky coat to a slanted backside, small head and scruffy spots. Any fictional hyena I may have come across likely played the role of antagonist.

Two days prior, we watched this female leopard sleep in a tree between two cubs that clambered over her and scrambled headfirst down the trunk. Her long forelegs and huge paws dangled down, one on each side of the branch on which her head rested, cheek against bark, her belly swelling to one side. Above her hung a pointed hoof and thin bone extending from a torso that I might have mistaken for a bird nest. Hyenas waited nearby for bones, which cats don't eat, to fall. Tonight she listened to mastication, lying in the grass, conserving energy; her cub batted at a moth; the hyena planted his foot on the heart of her kill and tore; we concerned ourselves with equity, but she did not need to eat.

This female had three cubs originally. One was reported dead two weeks ago; the second that we had seen so recently was now missing. How could she lie there? Why didn't she search? What sort of adolescent escapade was he on? I remembered a female raccoon whose baby was run over on the dead end street where I grew up. She sat in the high oak where I used to climb and wailed throughout the daylight hours, a wail to arrest the phases of the moon or inspire Michelangelo's *Pietà*. There was normalcy in that.

In the South African bush I wasn't perceived as human, and my perceptions shouldn't have betrayed me as such even to myself. I was a protrusion from a hunk of metal (a Jeep) that made a dull hum, which lions could use to mask their stalking of something else. That should have been enough, a minor connective thread to the web of territory and scent, eat, be eaten. I was paying top dollar for the human element to filter away—you don't want it as you listen to the coo of cape turtle doves, the ke-cha of a long-tailed shrike, the suck and splash of elephant legs in mud, the brush and stomp and crack of rhinos chomping grass and ripping branches, or as you hear the subterranean rumble of an elephant whose voice is largely in decibels too low for the human ear. You want to forget that here 19th century settlers contended with hippos and black mambas and lions as they tried to grow tobacco, wheat, and sugar on land plagued by locusts and droughts. You want to forget that here the British aimed Maxim .303 machine guns at a rag-tailed population of wily, independent Afrikaners and erected for them and their children the world's first concentration camps. You want to believe that an ecology in which red-billed oxpeckers sticking on the backs of buffalo and flickering in and out of the ears of giraffes to feed and symbiotically rid these animals of insects and ticks existed before human memory—but why?

Even here there was aberration. A week ago a coalition of five lions from an adjacent reserve wandered into the area. One of two dominant males of this territory fought them, killing one, scarring others.

We could see lines of dried blood like haphazard pencil marks across their backs and flanks. The four waited a few days, then tracked the dominant male and took revenge, an atypical impulse—or emotion—for lions. After the kill, still compelled by what we infer to be anger, they ate him, again an anomaly, though no more vicious in my mind than another sort of cannibalism that is expected: males eat cubs under a year old if not their own. Only then will the mothers—who have been pregnant, borne cubs, nursed and hunted for them—become fertile again, allowing the devouring males to perpetuate their own line. It is Darwinian, and the sacrifice of cubs is a given. I'm supposed to believe that bereavement, if it occurs, is immaterial, and that this singular incident of revenge and cannibalism was excessive, but who's to judge? It was as if the lions were in court demanding the death penalty for murder of a fellow gang member and taking it into their own hands when a mere life sentence was handed down. And the plot thickens: somewhere in the bush the other dominant male kept his pride while these four lazed in the sun, deceptively peaceful as teenage boys on a beach with a cooler of Coors. There would be another fight. For now, one lifted his huge head and licked behind the ear of another.

Churning out of a dry riverbed one night, the Jeep veered under overhanging limbs as four female lions padded up the road. They filed past us, nearly close enough for me to stroke, without turning their heads, without (it seemed) a glance. They held their heads low, forelegs and haunches gliding with slow, synchronized restraint. This was not a hunt, or not yet. We cut our headlights and turned off road after them, keeping them in a single spotlight as they wove through prickly acacias, our tires crackling over dry sticks and grumbling on loose stones. We didn't even whisper, though the lions wouldn't have cared. They led us to a clearing and continued across the open under an infinitely expanding hemisphere of stars. For an instant all life was out there in pulsing silver bolts of light and filmy white nebulae, which happened after thousands of years to reveal us, an odd speck of metal and breathless humans, and four female lions walking in steady single file towards their male. So camouflaged was he that without the females I would have missed him, with his dirt-brown coat and matted mane jutting in irregular clumps at the side of his heavy head. His paws were curled like those of a kitten, his head raised, eyes closed, a scar just visible between them. No golden Lion King he, yet his presence subsumed the arrival of the females who lay down in no particular order some yards away. Did he expect their return? Did he, the remaining dominant male, anticipate the four aberrant ones who might track him tonight, tomorrow, in a week? Was this languor transcendence or dull, dissociated ignorance—cause for dramatic irony that made me want to warn him, or not?

Beside the lion lay a prior kill, a fragile steenbok, its body excavated and once flighty limbs now no more than toothpicks tossed awry. Through my binoculars I caught its narrow face and wide-open eyes, which betrayed no presumption of death as perpetuating life, no consciousness of flesh and blood as offering, no salvation. I had no rationale for seeing something spiritual in this blatantly physical thing, this absence of self in dying.

Meanwhile, the lion would wait.

Under a noon sun in an open field, we shut off the Jeep. I hopped down and walked about ten yards to a watering hole until the guide said a crocodile could catch me in a second. So we stayed together, watched, and waited. First a few baboons skittered down to the edge, drank, and loped away. Then others followed, a crescendo of baboons leaping from surrounding trees, delousing one another, drinking, mewing, sunning. The smallest clung to the underside of the mother's belly as if toted in a Baby Bjorn. The largest male swaggered on his long front legs. If anything happened to him, another male, one of those hanging fruitlessly on the outskirts, would get a testosterone rush and grow, virtually overnight, bigger muscles and bigger penis, to assume control of the harem. Standing in a cluster some thirty yards away were six zebras swishing flies and munching grass. Their black and white streaks (which are so appealing) seemed to overlap from one animal to another, flattening perspective, and (antithetical to western thinking) masking individuality to enhance survival. They moved toward the water and drank, several at a time, then walked back out to the middle of the field, flicked their tails and nuzzled each other, or just stood. We might have left. We had a plane to catch that afternoon. But three giraffes appeared. They filled the horizon at the edge of the field, entering this orbit as if on cue from a conductor's baton, and froze, staring at us with huge eyes and long upswept lashes, scarcely exaggerated, it turns out, by Disney. All three were males, and they watched us with heads erect, very still, then slowly advanced, front and hind legs on one side moving together, then those on the other. One came to the edge of the water, stopped, then strode in slow motion to the opposite side. A second followed at a distance, the third stayed behind. I suppressed a cough until tears filled my eyes. The largest continued to stare, walk, stare, horns like candles, legs and neck far longer, proportionately, than I had drawn them as a kid. We didn't want to be responsible for his not drinking, but leaving was inconceivable.

And so we waited. An animal is most vulnerable when it drinks. And a giraffe has to hobble his forelegs till his knee joints stick out like a busted chair, and so much blood rushes down his neck that were it not for a valve his head would explode. You can tell a lot about a culture not by what it debates but by what it takes for granted. Water and the opportunity to drink it were not on that list here, nor are they in the township of Khayelitsha in Cape Town where more than two million live in corrugated tin, and proximity to a spigot is fortuitous. At home my dog expects water in his dish. I assume he will wag his tail when he sees me, and I assume furthermore that his behavior signifies happiness. How long we waited, I'm not sure, but we drank from our water bottles and whispered and savored the tension until that cathartic moment when the forelegs splayed, head went down only to pop up, then descend again, and the giraffe drank for, maybe, five seconds. I was tempted to see the whole scene as an orchestral score but resisted.

We flew out of the reserve in a bush plane low enough to still see scrubby trees, sandstone like gold pancakes, and strokes of green along rivers that didn't seem to move at all. No telltale signs of mongoose scurrying through grass or snakes unzipping a pond. All still, except us. We switched planes and flew south, and by the following afternoon we had driven a few hours and hiked out the rocky reach of the Cape of Good Hope. As we looked north the water was steely gray under clouds that half hid the sun, while to the south the same water was turquoise and scalloped in white. Even the clouds at their perimeter looked clean. After months of reading about the BP spill and flinching at shots of pelicans encased in oil on the front page of *The New York Times*, dreaming about corpses of whales shoved back to sea, and knowing that in ten years my unborn grandchildren would find oil when they went to build a sand castle, I stood on this promontory and relished a breezy, fickle illusion that the world is large. Let it be bigger, enough shrinking, enough feigning to understand. The water lurched and drew away and the tug of the horizon made me dizzy with relief. Staring 3,582 feet straight down, I thought about scurvy-ridden, dehydrated traders sailing carricks with square sails swelling and snapping in 75-knot winds, who may have spotted these cliffs if the moon were out, been drenched by an upsurge of froth and spit just as the ship hit an unrecorded, hull-splintering rock off shore. I thought of explorers before them, mistaking this continent for another, suddenly becalmed without water to drink as they followed the Southern Cross to the edge of a flat world. And I wanted to imagine the nights before these men, eons of water fingering crevices and falling back in the black congruence of the as yet unnamed, unbounded Atlantic and Indian Oceans. A day is only a day. By afternoon I stood in a craft store buying my daughter blue beads and a wood elephant to remind her of the Africa she has yet to see.

When I return to New York, I find a stray cat has given birth to three kittens in my back yard. She hides with them under a plastic box in which I store the garden hose and hisses when I come near. Soon the kittens glide through my ferns and pachysandra and stare at me with their yellow eyes. I've never liked house cats and have no intention of trying to keep them. My dog, who is both cowardly and well fed, sleeps in the sun and pretends not to notice when they pass by, stealthy as a dream. But I check my email daily for a message from our guide who promised to tell me the fate of the second leopard cub. I believed he would, being so responsible and well informed. For a long time I thought he might not know. My screen saver features the cub dozing on a limb. With her furled claws and fluff in her ears, I want to hold her. But I just look.

Missing

I'm considering taking down an ungainly splay-leafed maple in the back yard, which grows out of a rock with the tenacity of a hyena stealing kill from a leopard. This tree has left the pines behind it spindly and transparent with brittle branches reduced to naked twigs. It has caused the dogwood to grow sideways in search of the sun and bloom only on one side. It has made the growing of grass beneath its muscular arms a virtual impossibility. And yet? Without it, the dogwood might not right itself, the pines fail to flesh out. And the neighbor's new storm windows will simply stare. Besides, there is history. On steamy afternoons I welcomed the shade of this unlovely two-trunked tree, blessed the branches that enshrouded me and saved me the sight of the husky doctor who strutted on his deck in his underwear. I railed at tree surgeons for lopping branches I feared would not grow back, and I refused to pay their bills. Now I email my daughter about the dilemma and she responds—you want to take down the tree that had our rope swing? Mom, are you crazy? I tell her that tree went down years ago. She's here about once a month, so seeing tree ghosts is a story in itself, and psychologically significant, but doesn't solve the maple problem. Or maybe it does.

You get to a certain age and loss is a daily event—the dress that slipped off the hanger and lies askew on a pile of heels in the dim recess of the closet, the glasses you look for under the bed, in the other case, on the bathroom shelf, and find after the loss of a half hour on top of your head, or the desired item in the fridge you cannot even recall as the door stands gaping and you stand staring, seeking clues idiotically from a jar of mayonnaise. My daughter refers to these things as "mommy lost," fully assured of the finite nature of their absence. Nope, I assert, I'll never see that dress again. Looked everywhere. It's *gone.* We are in opposition: she believes a tree is there, which is

71

not, I believe a dress is not there, which is. Since I'm not by nature a pessimist, this must have something to do with youthful bright-eyedness and persistence vs. a mature assumption of the ephemerality of just about everything.

This assumption reared its head with the dismantling of my parents' house after fifty years (the haphazard labeling of items for auction, the stripping down of floral curtains, the tossing of painstakingly assembled photo albums, the rolling up of orientals) and grew to fruition with daily accounts of global disasters that shred human habitations in seconds: landslide in Colorado, earthquake in Yunnan, tornado in Oklahoma, wildfire in San Diego, flash floods in Arizona, tsunami in Indonesia. I see people on the 6:30 news shuffling through skeleton houses and mounds of cement and blown out toilets, picking up a flip-flop that survived, a doll's arm, a patch of a patchwork quilt, and those people always look at the camera in reeling disbelief and say well I'm thankful for my loved ones and we'll start again and all kinds of noble testaments to the resiliency of the human spirit. I guess you can't say much in a two-minute sound bite. In two hours could you say what it is to lose all the pictures of your kids, or the couch you just paid off, or the garnet earrings set in twirls of silver that belonged to your grandmother? They don't give you two hours, and there's a reason.

I lost my grandmother's necklace of baby sea pearls not to a natural disaster but to a crackhead who came through the skylight of my apartment building, ripped out two Medco locks, and took his time pawing through my underwear, stripping the bed, emptying coffee tins in the fridge and strewing clothes across the floor like the map of an alien planet. I was twenty-six and vulnerable. Twenty-six and violated. That loss was not entirely material, though in later years I sometimes thought the necklace would have enhanced a certain dress. Fleeting thoughts. Inconsequential, really. I never knew that grandmother, but I would see the necklace superimposed on pictures I had seen, she in her navy dress with V-neck collar, a Scottie on her lap, a small-brimmed hat cocked on her head, lips parting in a wry smile. She's the reason my mom had food on the table. Sometimes I would see the necklace locked in a dark drawer in a pawnshop on St. Marks and wonder what anyone thought it was worth.

Just a month after the apartment incident, I was ambling along 40th Street in Manhattan, lugging a briefcase and pocketbook and eating some yogurt. As the plastic spoon reached my mouth, the strap on my shoulder slid, jerked, pulled—yogurt splattered—and suddenly I was in a tug of war with a big woman in black jeans who yanked as if curbing a massive dog. I hung on like a Jack Russell terrier, purely overwhelmed by waves of indignation—how dare she? It's mine. So we pulled and tugged under a bald afternoon sun as heels clicked by and businessmen undoubtedly glanced our way. When I yelled at last, she ran, and I stood panting, the cheap bag dangling from my fingers. Some guy remarked I could really throw a punch, but I didn't know I had. I'd grown up in the age of peace and love and weighed as much as a dandelion. Still, the battle had been thrilling! Power coursed through my veins! Now I could call the police and set in motion the final revenge.

"Yes, I'm on 40th and this woman, she tried…"

"Did she get anything lady?"

"No, almost…"

The cop laughed and hung up, and I stood there in a phone booth feeling like a dust mite.

In subsequent weeks I had a story to tell, and I told it repeatedly, but friends looked at me as though I were high and said, so what if you lost your bag (which held about $10), you could've lost your *life*. I shrugged and conceded, knowing but never essentially feeling that they were right. It was never my own life I worried about losing except in childhood dreams.

I lost Nick McCallum when I was thirteen after wearing his ID bracelet for a year and sneaking out the window past midnight to walk around town with him and drink Coke. I lost the envy of those eighth grade girls, too. For days I sat on my yellow quilt listening to Smoky Robinson croon about the tracks of his tears while my own wore grooves in my soul. Staring at his photo, all affable smiles and ingenuous eyes, I could find no rationale and that was stunning. He had given no reason, simply walked away, literally, across the room at a party and that was that: a valuable initiation into meaninglessness and absurdity, which still I often failed to see simmering on the horizon in later years.

In a dreamy, disassociated state kids lose teeth, sweatshirts, notebooks, homework, North face fleeces, and—roughly proportionate to socio-economic bracket—iPhones and laptops. These losses rarely have an impact beyond the hassle of retrieving Sam's number, and no parent dealing with the financial consequences can applaud edenic obliviousness or transcendence, both of which could be survival tools in the face of lost friend, dog, grandparent, youth. People say loss makes one grateful for what one has, but a kid isn't going to like some other sweatshirt more because he lost the first and may, in fact, resent the remaining sweatshirt, which had not been worn for a reason. But what of the value of have-not-ness, the palpable insistence on absence as *something* unlike anything else, with its own barbs and ambiguities and labyrinthian tunnels? Forty years after the fact I safeguard the have-not-ness of Nick McCallum, which has nothing to do with *him*.

You get to a certain age and a season doesn't go by without a friend emailing about a failing, dying, or dead parent. Out come the pat phrases and palliatives: you were expecting this, right? Or, how sudden, but she lived a long life. She was in such pain, at least that's over. Or, I know you feel old now. But you shouldn't. Think young! The implication is getting over such loss is analogous to getting over a sore throat, which is expected to run the usual course of raspy throat to clogged nose to coughing of phlegm and then it's done. Death is the only certainty, not our symptoms in the face of it.

When my mother died eight months ago, friends wrote well-meaning letters that danced around that certainty, favoring reminiscences of life, mine and hers, and issuing bland gestures of sorrow over what they could not say. I don't know which is harder, reconceptualizing a lost person or lost years. One has finitude and unity, the other pointillist images borne loosely in a net submerged, a net full of whole years forgotten. When my children die, no one will recall my mother. Will that be her death, or is it now?

I know my mom made me who I am, to some extent, and I was a source of happiness to her, to some extent, in long years of decline and shrinking possibility. Beyond the significance of that reciprocity, her death, that certainty, brought only greater awareness of what I don't know. And so I keep asking.

What if I could believe death is a void you could paint with the oils of a life in just the appropriate hues and with just the appropriate heft without the mechanical echolalia battering inside and reminding me: ah, but then it would not be the void you know that it is, and it must be the void you know that it is—there will be no eyes gazing into a childhood dream of death.

What if you could believe all negative space is not a lack but a complement to what you have that is whole. *What if* when the moon is a marble crescent, the ash gray outline of the remainder caught your eye first, made your heart beat, made you mention to someone, the moon is bright tonight.

The Ghost Player

I

On a recent Saturday morning, wet snow clung to the curbs and crowns of trees while currents of warm air cloaked the streets and gnarled forsythia in fog. I was inside the local tennis bubble, gathering myself to serve when a gasp ushered from the next court, a grunt of muscle-mind exertion, a gritty slide of sole on Har-tru. A young guy was sidestepping at a lope, back and forth along the baseline. He charged to net, cut the air with a backhand slice from a precisely felt point over his left shoulder to a point mid-air out front before his right knee. He sidled back to the baseline ever so smooth, never taking his eyes from the opposite side of the court, leapt and swung, took his time setting up for an inside out forehand, tiny steps circling where a ball would bounce, racket face open to the court, anticipating. I continued to watch and he continued to hit for nearly an hour with no visible opponent and no ball. Each play he imagined and caused me to imagine. This was not a warm-up but a match. Dull lights in metal saucers dangled from the bubble covering the courts and wobbled slightly in a rush of wind outside. The giant white parachute with sea blue sides held; all was hushed except the occasional *skrit* of the ghost player's sneakers on grit. Who was winning? His face betrayed nothing, though sweat darkened his shirt between his shoulder blades, and I knew he knew.

Whoosh! He flicked open a can of balls. Again he danced like a boxer around a vortex, this time a gently tossed ball, and whacked a forehand to the opposite corner. Another ball rose overhead. His arm up-reached and I heard the smack of the racket strings as his wrist torqued and arm crossed his body—and I began to lose interest—the vitality of the stroke minutely and essentially diminished by a physical ball.

When I resumed my game, I'd lost all focus. I hit as if dreaming, seeing the ghost player in my mind's eye. In our microcosmic globe of polyester seamed by aluminum trusses, he sidesteps across the baseline, charges the net, chides himself, and sets his legs squarely to receive a serve. As growls of the local commuter train decrescendo, he prepares, his every move eerie and magnetic, because his is the most real opponent.

By the time I left the court the fog had drifted off and the sun, white hot and blurry in a winter vapid sky, bristled in the wet branches of a sycamore. I stared at it full on and thought of the moon on the other side of the earth, squinting through a clump of skyscrapers or sitting lightly as a sliver of honeydew on a table of glass.

That night I woke up suddenly at 3:10, hearing a crack and sizzle, the wind, maybe, spinning oak leaves and overturning trashcans. Out the window the highest, longest limbs were lunging and whipping the air into whirlpools, criss-crossing the moon and scarcely visible stars as if they could knock the brittle crescent out of the sky. I remembered two guys on a nearby court that morning who in two successive shots in the same point each broke their racket strings and marched off the court arguing about the score rather than marveling at the uncanny symmetry. It had seemed ludicrous.

Late that night, and often at night, I hear voices without sound (as the ghost player saw form without form) silent articulations of combat and confusion, words repeated with aching clarity until daylight finds them drained of color, limp as a dogwood petal tarnishing at the rim. My voice calculates the number of years I have left to live by any reasonable estimation, while the whisper of an other obliterates those words with breezy denial. Those obituaries one scans: died at 64, 72, 49, they are other lives, other diseases, other accidents. Flip the page, read about a fire. My other contends I will surpass them all. My other affirms the truth is a lie, a mirror wherein left is right and right is left. My other is as imaginary as a dragonfly cloud momentarily obscuring the moon.

II

When I was little I used to run races with my brother on the front lawn and play hide-and-seek long into the evening when fireflies startled the air and katydids chirred their little wings in a familiar rhythm we neither listened to nor cared about. Now the sound paints those nights and the tangy smell of cut grass and the slicked back grass under the sprinkler where we slid and shivered. Our parents would still be at the table, lingering over cigarettes and red wine, my mother's glass stained with ruby lipstick, my father tilting his saucer to pour back into his cup the coffee he had spilled. The black lab would bound after me, giving away my spot near a basement window hideout cloaked by pachysandra and ivy; the mutt would lie on the flagstone, too smart to retrieve balls, too independent to curry caresses behind her lopsided ears. In the gloaming we climbed a fence way back in the woods and played war in the neighbor's family graveyard, a square lot with headstones muffled by overgrowth, surrounded by a stone wall that became our ramparts, our watch towers.

Once my brother and his friend abandoned me there, telling me Indians had surrounded me and I could never escape. They had left a bow and arrow on the headstone of grandmother Vaux, and as night thickened they hooted and padded through the briars and swung on the beech limbs to make them creak. I peered over the wall and crouched again, quickly. I couldn't call, couldn't whisper. Faintly, a car revved and hiccupped as the driver shifted and popped the clutch. A sudden right time or inevitability or panic, heartbeat in the temples, impulse, or a yip from the lab, a sign. My hands flat on the top of the wall, I scrambled up and leapt—exposing my full self to arrows—and fled, never looking back.

Even younger, I'd sometimes wake up at night, needing to pee, and weigh the urge against the journey down the long hallway there and back lined on one side by a balustrade, the other by frame upon frame of black glass above my line of vision. Stealthily I pushed back the covers, tiptoed out of my room and down the hall, picking my way over notorious floorboards. I'd leave the bathroom door open, slowly unroll a few squares of paper, and slam down the seat against a witch who occupied the serpentine sewers below. Thump thump thump, I hurtled down the hall and leapt onto the bed, avoiding proximity to the cavern beneath, and touched my pillow, the safe zone. That lousy piece of foam rubber was safe.

"Oh," my mother would chortle from downstairs, "she's up."

"Twinkle toes," returned my father as he turned the pages of Evelyn Waugh.

The windowsill of the bathroom held a plastic habitat for my turtles, little ones that I won at fairs or picked up at the pet store. About the size of a silver dollar, the green shells with intermittent heads like pea shoots and old man legs would sit in the afternoon sunshine and sometimes crawl up an incline lined with mini plastic palm trees to the turtle castle that served no function since they couldn't fit through the door. They nibbled grains of turtle food and shortly died without cause. For each I held a funeral in the front yard at the margins of the lawn where grass conceded to a bed of mint and a flock of ferns. I wrapped the soft body in a wad of paper towel, placed it in an empty box of Milk Duds, and processed across the lawn, dog at my side, Teddy in my arms. I dug through the shallow fern roots and deposited my nameless turtles, one after another. I don't know why I kept trying. I knew they'd die, and I knew Teddy would not.

A small Steiff bear not much bigger than my hand, Teddy had charisma because he first belonged to my big brother, who had him for years. As my brother tried to grow up and assume the independence of a man, slinging his holster over the bedpost at night and hiding *Playboy* inside the covers of *Life*, he made the concession that Teddy could be mine during the day—but his at night. Teddy was benign, kind, cute, his chestnut hair and blond chest worn down like old sandpaper, one eye bright, the other hidden by tousled hair. He had a squeaker in his chest that had stopped squeaking and anyway seemed beneath him. I hated to let him go at night—how confusing being swapped back and forth as if his family were divorced.

"Teddy's okay with it," said my brother.

"Yeah, he's a stuffed animal," I retorted, knowing Teddy suffered in my absence.

Kids are generous in imbuing the inanimate world with life, not full-blooded-live-and-die life, but consciousness, as if it were a given that being and nonbeing co-exist in perfect fusion, that girl and bear mirror one another and look nothing alike, that the very *essence* of witch-dom can terrorize a three-year-old and abide by her rules. That was the beautiful asymmetry of the ghost player's game.

III

In the rational light of day, I still look for hints of consciousness in the most absurd places and listen for signs, like the distant car or dog yip that suddenly propelled my flight from the graveyard in the woods as a kid. A green arrow at the exit off the highway near my house lasts less than a minute, letting four cars through at most. When I miss it, I sit indignantly while cars hurtle past, rocking my car as the blinker clicks and clucks with irritating regularity. If I make the light while cruising at 60, barely slowing as I swing into the turn, I anticipate auspicious consequences for me or someone I love, and for a flickering instant I deeply believe the light is complicit. Although it's all timing (and a bathetic substitute for abrogating witches), hope serves a satisfying ace to the evidence that would counteract it.

But how quickly the score shifts, and the players switch sides. Certainty goes to live wherever eons of mute birthday wishes drift disembodied beyond the feathery rise of snuffed-out candles. And whatever forces are at play again became as entangled as lovers in summer sheets, one leg crooked over a thigh, an elbow flung overhead.

For years I had a boyfriend who lived 3000 miles away. Since he was always broke or getting degrees, our love lay in the letters that flew from coast to coast over wheat fields and silos, shopping centers littered with abandoned carts and Burger King cups and guys hawking crystal meth. From my self-conscious scribbling, he honed fictions that were frayed, wishful, and definitive. He saw me striding along Avenue A at 4 a.m. just to see who was on the street. He saw me in maroon, hands in my pockets, catching my reflection in a store window, or in velvet the color of mangoes at a box at the opera. I tried to disabuse him of all this. Just working my day job, I'd say. When he finally came east, we sat in a bar, my eyes on the dark hairs on his fingers that lingered around a glass of scotch. But I felt him stare head-on as he said his best friend had shot himself in the head, that he'd found him in a wicker chair, chin on his chest one afternoon when he ambled in, musing about me. He lit a cigarette with a flick of his lighter, and smoke passed over his freckles and Aegean-blue eyes. I don't think he told me to remember his friend (whom I didn't know) or to puzzle over why because he never knew and maybe no one did. But he wanted to see my lips part, or my hands flinch, or my eyes say nothing with all the precision and timing he had imagined when I, partner and opponent, was missing.

Slippery as a Salamander,
Shifty as Light

Back in college I came to the city to visit a guy from school. I wasn't into him, exactly, at least not yet, but he had a place to crash, a mattress on the floor in an apartment in New York City. His roommate slept on a foldout in the living room and talked a lot about chugging brewskies and dancing to disco. My friend was a little more earthy in his flannel shirts and used jeans, his fine bangs flopping over his wire rims. He listened to Miles Davis and played recorder and sax. That's why we went to hear jazz at the West End somewhere uptown. In those days, the '70s, the place had a music room next to the bar with its gritty booths and lumpy fries. We wedged past the crowd and got a table about ten feet from the amps. Joe Jones ambled in, sat down at the drums, and adjusted the mike. As we started in on our pitcher of Bud, he teased us with a few beats and ripples of the cymbals. "Always like playing the Apple," he growled, and the room exploded. Couples nodded to each other, guys at the bar hooted, waitresses in jeans and black T-shirts skimmed between tables with ten brimming glasses on a tray, and a crowd swelled at the door. This was it. Reality, hot and pure.

The next memorable dose came a summer later when I went off to Europe for my cultural education and wound up living in Athens with a Greek dancer. There I was in my lavender wrap-around, fresh out of Philadelphia's Main Line, sitting in a taverna with a friend and watching this guy in tight black pants and white shirt that couldn't button across his chest. He spun and knelt, cigarette in his mouth, shoulders tensed, each movement flowing with sturdy certainty into the next. He slapped his boots, looked only at me, and the sweat bled through his shirt under the arms and across his back.

My friend met a Dutch guy and went off to Sardinia, leaving me free to frequent Theodore's taverna and walk around Plaka with him, hand in hand, me the chosen one, a tourist no longer. His sister worked night shifts at a hospital so we used her apartment, which I figured was OK with her. Curled on the couch one morning, I awoke to a nasal barrage of expletives. Marianne was pacing with her hands on her broad hips and her elbows thrust forward like a disconcerted swan. Back and forth her fierce heels clacked the tile floor as she swept up Theodore's shirts, pants, photo album and English dictionary and dumped them into the hall.

"That's my sister! Village mind," Theodore fumed. We spent a few days looking at notices on telegraph poles. Then he led me to his new place, a boxy little room with one burner in the corner and a small fridge. The best feature was the verandah where we'd sit at night watching lights flick on and off in the four-story apartments. With his feet propped on the railing, Theodore would call to the women as they hung out their laundry. I studied the Greek dictionary, listened to stray cats, figured I'd found heaven.

Mid-July was festival time in his village in Central Greece, and I would be the first American to stay there, he said. The bus churned from Athens with radio blaring and windows sucking in the blazing wind. It dumped us (portentously) at a crossroad. From there we walked a few miles, my slate-blue American Tourister in hand, kicking up dust and listening to the jangle of goat bells. When we reached the village, Theodore pointed to an empty plot—"Mine someday. I'll build a house with a floor, with water, refrigerator, television."

His parents' house had three rooms, no bathroom, a dirt floor, and an open fire beneath a clay oven. While Theodore drove the tractor around and his father played backgammon, Mana paraded me through the village, arm in arm, stopping at houses where old women eyed me up and down, called me skinny and shook their heads gravely while offering me plates of cookies dusted in sugar. Mana would give me two chicken breasts while she gnawed on the stringy neck. Or we had starlings that Theodore shot. Their whole bodies floated like unborn chicks in orbs of oil, oregano, and gamy broth.

For two nights, all night, oboes, drums, violins, and clarinets whined through the village, and families clustered at tables in the square. Theodore's grandmother chuckled and lit the young men's cigarettes. Everyone linked arms, turning and sidestepping in a serpentine behind the guy who bobbed and ducked and twisted as he led, handkerchief in hand. A man in torn pants reeking of urine mumbled to himself and staggered in and out of the chain, but no one objected. I was impressed.

Sometimes we sat out on the family's porch and Theodore propped a black and white TV in the window. It was the only one in the village, and anyone strolling by could stop and watch. Children squatted on the steps, pointing and giggling at near naked women. The guys hooted at Cadillacs and Maseratis.

"I want a beeeg car to drive through the village!"

"They're noisy and dirty," I returned.

"No, a car means much money. That is every Greek man's dream."

"In America the air smells bad, the highways are clogged."

"Maybe I'll go to America. Come back with a hat and black car and fat cigar," Theodore swaggered across the porch like a Texan.

"I'd rather have a donkey."

He whirled around, slapped his leg, and whistled. "She wants a donkey! You are crazy, very crazy."

I didn't care what he said. My prior life had paled. White suburbia lay far away under a filmy piece of Saran Wrap. I'd found something *authentic*.

I might have lived in the Greek village, sitting by the well and gossiping about Basil's sister who was up to no good in Athens. Or I might have stayed on the Kenai Peninsula and taken up salmon fishing. Right after high school I went up to Alaska with two other girls and settled for a week or so on a hillside overlooking Cook Inlet. At night we lay under a piece of plastic tied to four trees and rain slanted in at any side and mosquitoes amassed on the netting we wrapped around our heads. At twilight the skyline of mountains became two dimensional and close. But I wanted to get *in* them, *on* them, so I asked a fisherman to take me across the bay and told my friends if I didn't come back in a week to come look for me. He and I puttered over the water, dipping like a heartbeat, not too sure what to say to each other, and though the sun persisted at that latitude, a stray cloud could bruise the water, turning it from dancing azure to purplish black. On the opposite shore were two mute houses, no road, no trail. No problem. I trudged into the overgrowth, admiring fantasy-size ferns and clambering over fallen trunks like a kid in a playground. I don't know if I made ten yards before it poured. Cocooned in my sleeping bag, I hunched against a massive cedar and battled black flies for my cheese sandwich. The grizzlies that owned those woods never lumbered into my thoughts. The sun just hung in the treetops on a pearly sky so I didn't know when it was day again, but after a span of almost dreams, I lurched down to the shoreline again and sat there chucking stones in the water, half defeated.

"I thought you'd be back," chimed a woman in purple rubber boots. She knew. I didn't need to say a thing. She took me in for a few nights—Beth, a nurse from Iowa, and Slim, her husband, who left the family farm in Kansas when he was seventeen and wound up here, lean and leathery, rocking in his handmade rocker and reading Robert Service. We ate moose steaks from the deep freeze and celebrated their adopted Eskimo son's sixteenth birthday with sake. I climbed a ladder to sleep in the attic whose pitched roof prevented me from standing. There I lay with upturned face discerning eyes in the knotty ceiling boards and hearing pointillist plunks of rain that amassed to a din. They had chosen this other life for reasons I'd never know. I might have. At that time, simpler seemed realer. I wanted to see elemental life made visible, like the skeleton of a trout on an empty plate.

Instead, I made my way home, taking an elliptical path like the salmon that navigate two thousand miles up the Alaskan coast and south again to a natal stream guided by migratory cues. The fish orient themselves to the earth's magnetic field through tiny electrical charges in ocean currents. Figuring out where my cues came from was more problematic.

Slim and Beth and I exchanged Christmas cards for a few years until I lost their address.

I have boxes of slides of the mountains of Alaska. No people, not one. Slides of angry black mountains at night, glaciers muscling over rock, crags where people died, mountains in violet light.

A lot depends on the frame of the camera you're looking through, your zoom potential and choice of lenses, at least I used to think so. I spent most of college trying to figure out whether the "thing" out there existed at all, or relied on my perception of it, which resulted in a sort of artsy pomposity and way too many photos of the insides of flowers and such. Then I found out it had to do with belief, or maybe sex.

My best friend in elementary school was a girl named Didi, who lived in Gladwyne and rode horses. I spotted her on the first day of kindergarten, petite in her bobby socks and crinoline, her bangs cut straight across. I felt lumpy and big in my plaid dress, so maybe that's why I chose her. Anyway, we grew up cantering around my house, leaping over broomstick jumps, drawing families of horses, and spying on my big brother and his cute friends. She was an artist and an actress with a voluminous appetite for life and French toast. She could never get enough and she could never get fat. I lost her to a boyfriend in high school and while she did whatever she did with him, I decided to find out who I was by writing poems and smoking pot.

Years passed, and my literary endeavors landed me in a cubicle in New York reading the slush pile for a publisher. I used to walk to and from my office on Fifth Avenue and my apartment on the Upper West Side, cutting through the park where I often spotted a white-haired couple on bikes dressed completely in purple—tie-dyed purple T-shirts, purple shades, purple caps. I wondered how they'd found their touchstone of commonality, and whether they ever argued at Altman's over shades of purple. In those days Hare Krishnas often fluttered along Madison Avenue like exotic orange birds, those white suburban boys in monk robes and sandals. They looked so pale, and I wished they'd grow their hair and listen to rock 'n roll and stop handing me pamphlets. One day a doughy girl in a loose tan shift approached me with an armful of carnations and Mars bars. Having no use for either, I nearly swept by when I realized it was Didi. She had seen me, I had to stop. For a moment we stared at each other. I took off my shades and fumbled in my bag for the case. "Didi, I can't believe it. So what are you doing?"

"Call me Diane now, OK? I'm living in New York for awhile." She took a deep breath and looked me right in the eye. I began to regret the shades. "Oh, Caroline," she intoned, "I've found it, you can't imagine." I didn't want to imagine. She looked terrible, her once honey hair pulled back in a greasy ponytail, her silky skin covered in pimples, her green eyes, dull and hazel. For weeks afterward she would appear outside my apartment, intent on selling me a subscription to her newspaper, which would save the world. Finally, we had coffee at a place near my office. The egg salad sandwich caught in my throat as she produced diagrams of the universe with a sprinkling of aphorisms that she'd copied down while confined to a single room without sleep for three days. "Do you remember science class in eighth grade?" Diane said. "Do you remember Mrs. Whetstone who used to say, 'Oh, Didi, you ask too many questions.'" (God, little Mrs. Whetstone in her tight skirts and high heels, with her secret notebook and orange hair that bristled like SOS.) "Well, now Reverend Moon has answered all my questions." Diane was appeased; I was skeptical. Some incarnation of "it" had propelled Jack Kerouac across country eight times, had lured me to dives in New York where crack addicts floated by like ghosts, had left me in a sodden sleeping bag curled up like a wolf, and just evaded me as I stared at a starling in a bowl of soup. I had hungered for the extraordinary; she had been swallowed by it. I had looked for something definitive in the echolalia of the madman at the festival in Greece; she had found it in Moon, and the result seemed to me maddeningly limited rather than liberating, as if one had always to wear purple, as if one could not choose whom to love.

The omniscient Moon also provided a husband. A few years after our lunch I received an engraved invitation on thick parchment in a large envelope that contained another envelope, the customary sort for coming out parties and weddings on Philadelphia's Main Line. Diane's family had moved to an estate far out in the countryside, past

Malvern, and the wedding was to occur in an Episcopal church followed by a reception at the house. I managed to miss the wedding but make the reception, a serene affair on a terrace overlooking the rolling hunt country of Chester County. I wandered among turquoise silk and yellow chiffon, nibbled watercress sandwiches and caviar canapés, sipped Chablis and tried to read the thoughts of Didi's mother, who seemed to own herself as well as twelve acres, standing there poised in pink, her shoulder-length hair in a page boy style, her waist still trim within the Kelly green sash. She might have been pleased. At least there was ceremony. Diane hustled out the glass door when she saw me, hugged me, thanked me for coming, and tugged my hand to lead me to Hikaru who was standing alone and glassy eyed. He extended his hand, bowed, nodded. With such a broad smile and square jaw, I sort of expected him to say something, but we just kept smiling and nodding. It was a little strange.

"He can't speak any English! His parents are farmers in Japan! Oh, I went there. They eat at this low table with a heater underneath. There's no central heating. It's so interesting!"

"Sounds great."

"We're going to be married and it's going to be ideal."

"Didn't you already get married?"

"Oh, this? No. This is just for them." She nodded towards the hundred or so guests drifting through the gardens with highballs wrapped in cocktail napkins, the ice cubes clinking gently. "The real wedding is in Madison Square Garden in two weeks. There will be five hundred other brides."

My mind was rapidly computing the number of Moon devotees this occasion would produce when Didi drew close and whispered in my ear. "We haven't consummated the marriage yet. I mean, we're not *really* married."

I wanted to take her by the shoulders and shake her, this little girl from Gladwyne, whose childhood had been washed away except dimly, in another life, the words of Mrs. Whetstone and our galloping and galloping in circles, this girl who had yet to wake up to a life that would feel like faded corduroys, Dear Didi whose parents may or may not still have believed they were giving her a wedding to remember, a wedding to fulfill the slippery dreams on which she was raised.

I used to sit on my daughter's bed reading her *Beauty and the Beast* and *Cinderella*, stories in which real life lessons (greed and envy lead to spinsterhood) mingle seamlessly with fantasy (correct foot size is the ticket to a prince). When we talked about these tales, I didn't distinguish much between the two—my daughter grew up both selfless and romantic—and perhaps one shouldn't, given the exceptions to the distinction on both counts. Greed has its payoffs and princes may really like small feet.

My daughter is twenty now and has her own stories. I listen one afternoon as I watch her sort old clothes. Sunlight pours in, bathing the windowsill and a pink silk elephant perched there on his haunches, the light as it shifts transmuting threads of rose to purple and cinnamon. Not long ago I brought him as a gift from Thailand, having snipped off the label: Made in China. I call him Babar; she insists on Ganesh—we smile at the incongruence and leave it at that. She tells me that a girl at her university had a boa constrictor. This pet was six feet long and routinely ate small mammals. It roamed freely in her room, curling neatly in the corner around novels by Henry James and poems by Sylvia Plath. The girl adored her snake and called him pet names like Zingo and Lance. Some months into the school year, the boa lost his appetite. He languished on the rug, showing no interest in life or even small bunnies set fetchingly before him. At last, fully distraught, the girl took him to the vet who questioned her at length about the boa's behavior. She described his lassitude, his disinterest in food. By now he had not touched a living thing in more than a week. She wondered how long his sleek body could last; she worried that his ruddy colors had paled, his skin lost its marvelous elasticity.

And does he sleep at night?

Oh yes. He stretches out alongside me in bed.

Straight out, uncoiled?

Yes, it's comforting to feel him there.

The vet demurred before looking her in the eye. He's in a state of preparation. He has to empty himself completely to make room. He lies beside you because he's sizing you up.

My daughter breaks down laughing, and I shriek, "I can't *believe* the university let her have a boa. I can't believe he was loose."

She shrugs and looks at Ganesh. "It's true, I swear, it's unreal."

Circling the Pond

Once a day my mother walks around the goose pond. When I'm with her, I do the same. We call the terrier, put the red leash in my pocket, and search for my mother's cane. Outside, she sees a cloud and asks that I go back for her rain hat. At ninety she still gets a perm every three months, her hair washed and set every week. We are prepared.

This particular June day is cool and dry. She takes small steps, watching where she plants her snowy New Balance sneakers. Although the slope from her apartment to the pond is gentle, the retirement community has laid a serpentine path that decreases the incline by a good fifty degrees. It makes the walk longer too. I watch my feet to avoid the goose droppings; my mother flicks them aside with her cane. "All this shit," she says. I'm surprised to hear the word escape her red lips. The geese are a major source of contention here, on par with national debates about offshore drilling and gay marriage. The green contingent wants to live and let live. They disregard the shit and love the geese. They say once you start the genocide there's no telling where it will stop. The opposition dreads the green-brown smears across the sidewalks, fears for the safety of their small dogs, and develops insomnia as a result of goose honking. It's the age-old romantic/realist dichotomy, and everyone knows who's on which side. The authorities skirt the issue by surreptitiously stealing goose eggs, but my mother knows how to get those people talking.

"Poor mothers lay one and come back, gone," I say.

"That's how it is," she says.

We pass a couple seated on a bench who gaze across the driveway into a tangle of trees and vines.

"You're looking well today," my mother remarks.

93

The old lady chimes, "How could I not? I'm watching finches and sitting next to the handsomest man in town."

The handsomest man does not visibly register the remark, or anything. His hairless arm rests on the arm of the bench.

"Who's that cheerful lady?" I mutter to my mother.

"I have no idea."

We nose along a stretch of driveway that brings us within ten yards of the pond. A fountain at the center sucks in water and sprays it in a circle. You can hear it from my mother's apartment, so I always think it's raining. White drops, luscious life drops, momentarily aloft, pour into the pond. Five years ago the surface was deep slate. Now it's green with yellow swizzles. "Is that algae?" I ask. "Why does it look like that?"

"That's this place," she shrugs.

We get closer to the pond. "Everyone's out today," notes my mother. Four hundred and fifty people live in the Quadrangle retirement community. So far we've seen nine. A black attendant is standing at the pond's edge watching the geese. Behind him on a bench slumps a man with his arm in a cast who stares at his lap. He wears a beret and a brown cardigan. After circling the pond, we see both men are still there and neither has moved. "He's got problems," says my mother.

We leave the pond side and push on. We breast a hill and my mother stops, ostensibly to bellow at her dog who is snuffling in someone's pachysandra; she is breathing loudly, as if she were asleep, just a bit quicker.

"I'm *interested* in the color of your toenails," she says to me. She lowers her head for closer scrutiny.

I glance at my bunions and cusps of magenta cushioned in Naots. "I know. Beautiful." She has passed on the art of circumlocution; it has taken years.

Due to the glorious weather, we decide to take another loop around the pond. Some grandchildren are playing by the water, tossing pebbles at the geese, and my mother pauses to watch. Five stains decorate the front of her rosy floral blouse, and I consider telling her. I don't want her to feel *old*, but she'd be mortified if she went to dinner in that.

"If you didn't have a dog, you probably wouldn't walk so much," I comment.

"Of course not," she snaps. With her head down, she forges on. The morning sun threads through her hair and shines on her pink scalp. Descending the final incline, she wobbles and I grab her arm. She pulls away. "I'm *fine*."

"You said when you hit ninety you'd let me help."

"Well, what do you think I do when you're not here?"

"But I'm here."

"Now."

I turn my attention to the dog. A man is coming our way swinging his cane like a golf club. "Get her on the leash," my mother commands. "That man will get a real hate on." I squat down, inviting the terrier over, but she charges past me after a squirrel. The man cocks his head to view a hawk circling above. It, too, expects baby geese. He passes us without a word, going clockwise around the pond.

When we get back to my mother's apartment, the screen door wheezes as I open it. "Go ahead," my mother mutters, directing me with her cane. Inside the air is thick. Smells of new carpeting and hair spray and burnt toast have coalesced like sedimentary rock. Neatly arranged in a square, around the square glass coffee table, are a sofa and three armchairs. The ladies who come to drink martinis on Monday nights have trouble getting out of them. I may have to get stiffer chairs, my mother says. Hanging in her three windows are chintz curtains from our old house, cut to fit the new size. Everything, in fact, is from the old house. Certain patterns hold, like the painting of Naples centered over the sideboard between two brass candlesticks. When she sold the house after fifty years, she sold off furniture and gave some to me. The really nice bureaus and orientals made the cut, first to a large apartment, then to this one. Sometimes I see these spaces inside each other like Russian nesting dolls.

When I leave the Quadrangle, my mother always walks down the hall with me and stands by the window while I throw my stuff in the trunk. I see her ruddy complexion and halo of white hair as the sun ricochets off the glass. I wave, she waves. How small she looks, quite suddenly. I pull out of lot six, drive straight through the stop sign in the driveway, over the speed bump, and right onto Darby Road, Haverford, Pennsylvania, USA.

When I arrive home in New York, my dog lifts his head nonchalantly and gets up to scratch behind his ear. He sits there, legs planted far apart, and stares at me. We both know he needs a walk. I toss the contents of my suitcase in the hamper and pass through the house, opening windows. A red light is flashing on the phone. "It's . . . your cousin Karen!" chirps the message with a lilt, like a talk show host introducing Loretta Lynn. "I know it's been awhile and I hope you won't think I'm interfering, but I have some thoughts about your mother." She used up the rest of my recording time with her calendar for the week and a blessing from God. That can wait. I go to a local track and run around it eight times with my iPod on shuffle at ear-damaging volume.

Karen went to the Quadrangle recently for lunch and has concluded that my mother should not be driving. She noted a bill ready to be mailed that had no stamp. In addition, the address did not appear in the window of the envelope. I know what my mother would say. If Con Edison doesn't get paid, they won't be shy about asking again.

I call my brother in Wisconsin.

"Well, *I'm* not going to take away the keys," he says.

"Me either."

"Let's have the doctor tell her next time she goes."

"He's scared of her too."

Weeks pass. I picture my mother plodding toward her VW and opening the door for the terrier. She uses back roads to avoid the lights though time could not be the reason. She knows these roads. She used to walk them as a little girl, two miles to school and back again, holding her English nanny's hand. Later, she drove them and drove fast, accruing so many speeding tickets when I was a teenager that she lost her license and had to take a remedial course. Now she drives haltingly, pressing the accelerator and releasing it, pumping and gliding, lurching and checking—I don't know how the terrier can stomach it. She makes her way to an Italian market to get gooey, expensive cheese and bruschetta for the Monday night martini group. Or she drives to her alma mater, Bryn Mawr, where the students exclaim, "Cute dog!" and she replies, "Yes, she is." She used to get these students talking about this and that. She'd learn what they ate for breakfast and what they thought about the Haverford guys and the president of the college, who is not an alum. Now she calls back the dog as if she were an annoyance, though she knows she's not, and chats to her instead. On these days she doesn't walk around the pond; the terrier has had a good outing.

I call every few days to make sure she's okay. She has fallen more than once and refuses to carry a cell phone. She keeps me posted on the goose wars and Lynn's alcohol consumption and Martha's disease that will last a year. Poor Martha, she's taking steroids and has blown up like a balloon.

"The doctor says I should take a driving course," my mother says.

I feign surprise. "Oh? Probably a good idea."

"Ridiculous."

"Why don't you look into it?"

"At my age, if I have an accident, so what?"

"But what about the other guy?"

She doesn't respond.

Someone could sue her for all she's worth, but I don't want to say that or she'll think I'm after her money. Later she tells me the course costs three hundred dollars and isn't worth it. She adds, "Your brother says my driving is a *moral* issue."

"Uh-huh." We wait like fencers in position. If anyone took my keys away, I'd fight, just as I did when someone tried to grab my bag in midtown Manhattan back in the crack days when such things were a common occurrence. I see the circumference of her existence shrinking like a lariat when you give it a good tug. I also see a little girl running blindly into the street after her Frisbee. I don't know how to weigh the two, a certainty and a possibility, though I should.

"Did the doctor test your reflexes?"

"I guess so. I had to catch a ruler."

"How'd you do?"

"I don't know. I didn't ask."

But I already know. An eighteen-year-old would catch the falling ruler after eight inches, a forty-five-year-old after fourteen. My mother's score was twenty-four. What could happen in that twenty-four-inch time/space equation? Just how vast was it, what broken limbs and lives could it contain? The doctor had made no comment. We were passing around this task like a tray of rancid shrimp cocktail.

A month later she and I are walking around the goose pond. A willow bows over the surface. With each languid gust, its tips comb through the thickening algae, leaving temporary marks of dark water. The sun is pale and hot today, too hot for the residents. Behind closed windows the air conditioners are humming, eating up moisture, and stabilizing body temperatures.

Maybe she'll have a stroke and I won't have to talk about driving, I think, but that sounds as though I want her to have a stroke, which I don't. Or maybe the car will give out and she won't think it's worth saving, but that won't happen either and if it did, she'd buy another. She got this one at age eighty-six, along with a puppy. But when I tell her she'll live to a hundred, she says, God, I hope not.

"Katherine says she's really going to do it," reports my mother. "She's trying to convince her twin sister."

"Do what? Go to Europe?"

"Why, kill herself," she retorts, stating the obvious. Her New Balance sneakers proceed, the whole sole coming down flat with each step.

"How?"

"Pills. They've been saving up since February. I'm the only one who knows."

"Are you going to tell a nurse?"

"Why should I?"

"Maybe she wants you to or she wouldn't have told you."

My mother shakes her head. "She knows I'll keep it to myself, unlike *some* people here." She waves her cane toward the apartment above hers. "Now if *she* finds out, well, it's all over."

"So which one is Katherine?"

"Former professor of psychology at NYU, very well known, I mean nationally. She started the Monday night group. But after two martinis she gets very quiet."

My mother walks up the serpentine path. I cut up the incline, dodging worms of guano hardening in the sun. The terrier pants behind us and lies down in the shade, the overgrown grass concealing her front paws and half of her head. Her sharp ears stand up, little white pyramids in the sun.

"Your geraniums are beautiful."

"Yes, they're rather nice, but the impatiens are a mess." I wouldn't have described them that way, but then my mother has high standards. She pokes them with her cane. We linger for a minute in the sun while her chest heaves. We used to be the same height, but over the past few years, she has shrunk four inches. She still stands straight, having learned good posture as a girl by carrying books on her head. With her broad back and straight hips, she's solid from top to bottom, like a cylindrical D battery. She always wears long sleeves because she thinks big arms are unsightly. I don't have her brand of vanity.

"Wait here," says my mother. I kneel by the potted plants, trying to resurrect the stems, while she descends the hill and joins a lady who looks like a spider with her frail arms and black dress and tiny feet. My mother walks alongside her, never touching her arm, though the woman does not look up or around her. They walk halfway around the goose pond, then my mother peels off, waves, and trudges up the path as usual. A large goose with goslings in tow rustles its wings, extends its neck, and charges the terrier. My mother yells and swings her cane. The terrier barks, tail up, ears forward. There will be blood.

The next day a few of the oldest women talk quietly as they pass in the hall. The authorities are trying to seal up the incident, but my mother knows whom to talk to. She is part of a sticky and tenuous web connecting Katherine to several ladies in discrete buildings in the community. Katherine confided in Eleanor, who told a nurse, who showed up at the designated hour and confiscated the pills, which belonged to the women.

End of story? No, says my mother. She'll try again. After all, she fought to wear pants, smoke, vote, go to college, get a doctorate, and teach. Now she's blind. She's ninety-*five*. She can't do anything, not even this.

"I wouldn't have ratted," I say. My mother raises her eyebrows. We are sitting on her sofa, which is covered by a white sheet. The terrier sits at the opposite end. She is deeply attached to my mother but keeps her distance. "Listen," she says. "There's something I want to say—I've been waiting to say it for a few weeks." My heart becomes a tangible presence, and my eyes fail to blink. The grandfather clock che-chinks. One lid droops; she taps her foot on the oriental. I watch her as I did when she caught me sneaking out a window or forgetting to set the table. "I know you called the doctor behind my back. Let me tell you, if you have something to say to him, you tell me first. Got it?" She doesn't wait for an answer. "All this fuss. Driving, reflexes. Well, I'm not there yet."

She gets up to take a walk and calls the terrier. Rain is bouncing on the surface of the pond. The fountain has been shut off, revealing a skeletal metal spout. I don't know if I'm supposed to go along, and I don't ask. She starts off, walking clockwise around the goose pond, her head down, planting her sneakers and measuring the slope with her cane. Years ago, when my mother took naps, my father would admonish me in a raspy whisper to be very quiet. He would even take off his shoes.

I return to New York, and several weeks slip by as serenely as a swan on water. I sit at my kitchen table rifling through the Travel section and talking to my mother on the phone. She says that the weather has been muggy and that Katherine is in a coma and her sister is in intensive care but expected to recover. They've been placed in separate hospitals, which is cruel. She has driven to Bryn Mawr several times to see the sister, who says she's glad she didn't take quite enough to do the job. The sister doesn't get too many visitors since the Quadrangle is not making any announcements about this. Most of the residents won't notice they're gone until they return, if they do.

Whoever comes back will be moved to a single room in the assisted living building where she can be watched. The twins had already removed the art from the walls of their apartment and given away all their furniture except two chairs.

III

Questionable Paternity

4/11/09: Bush emerged today from isolation to be photographed with nubile cheerleaders in Waco. Obama is shopping for a church, and hungry ministers are casting their nets. "Washington Churches Eye a Prize," writes the Times, *and I mark the emphatic assonance. The competition is frenzied. And Jesus will rise tomorrow.*

When my daughter was five she had a crush on God. I taught her the Lord's Prayer, and she prayed for me and her stuffed animals. But she wanted to go to church, especially on Easter. We shopped around for a while, finding at least ten Presbyterian churches within a square mile and not a single Episcopal one. Since I insisted on choirs, incense, Latin, and Gothic clerestory, we joined a church an hour away, which meant getting up on Sundays at 7, ironing my son's khakis and my daughter's lacy rose dress, sitting with a congregation of tweedy people whom we didn't know and who, snapped my husband, were pious today and firing people the next. The church was nestled in Sleepy Hollow, all stone and stained glass, the pews of dark wood, the cushions red and plush. It was smaller than my childhood church and a little too friendly. After the service you shook the minister's hand and convened in a room replete with sweets, unbounded sweets, and my stocky children were in heaven, sampling with abandon cupcakes and muffins, banana breads and Danish. The daisy-white congregation reached out to us and mid-week to the poor. Each Sunday the minister listed the names of people in the community who had died and were watching over us from a happier place, which was too creepy for words. I stopped going although my daughter said God would be mad. Today, at age twenty-two, she blames her agnosticism on me, and she has every right. After dropping out of church, I read her Bible stories and discussed the metaphorical implications of getting spat out alive from a whale's belly and diverting a river bed before the invention of bulldozers. But this was bland fare compared with the soprano harmonies of "Hark the Herald Angels Sing," the sapphire stained glass ablaze above the nave, the processions, the dusky smell of incense hovering like angels among the ancient shadows. She liked putting on her patent leather shoes and white tights, making crosses out of crisp palm leaves, kneeling when everyone else did, closing her eyes tight and trying to guess when to open them again. God would help her out if elementary school got tough. By middle school He was losing visibility.

Her experience of infatuation and loss was familiar. When I was a kid, Easter brought chicks and coconut eggs in a nest of synthetic green, licorice jelly beans, a yellow spring coat, and a straw bonnet decked with daisies worn once and readily shed for jeans and flannel shirts. Scratches on the side of the grandfather clock were, I believed, irrefutable proof of the bunny that had delivered the goods. Our stomachs churning with chocolate, we left the sunshine behind and blinked in the dim vaulting of a stone Episcopal church. The organ struck, we rose. With lace on my socks and earnest heart teeming, I belted out "Jesus Christ is risen today . . ." With what solemnity and grace I undertook the long Alleluias! With what empathy I beheld the stigmata! But beneath the smocking of my dress, my heart whispered, how could a father let this happen? How could three days on a barren hill, nails ripping through your flesh, save anyone? And what about the other two hanging there? And what did it mean to be saved? Some girls had new spring coats and others didn't. Some people had stone mansions and horses, others put PONY at the top of their Christmas list and hoped for the best.

Still, I loved the medieval lanterns hanging from chains, the cataracts of lilies in great bundles on either side of the altar, the cool crease of the cushion when I knelt with bare knees, the red hymnals with easy-to-read hymns, the stiff prayer book with its icy thin pages. When I'd been confirmed and was old enough to take communion, the top of my head would tingle as the minister tipped the chalice and sweet thick wine stuck in my throat. I felt proud to be humbled; I felt lonely to be secretly in touch with *something*. My parents never took communion. In fact, on days other than Easter, they dropped me off at church. That seemed normal. Mothers dropped us at school, the skating rink, the smoky house of the piano teacher whose windows were occluded by yellow shades. For a while I got dropped off with God.

I didn't expect our relationship to be finite, one never does, but something vanished like a sock in the laundry that leaves the other bereft. I don't experience a cardinal rising of the spirit when tulip tips nudge through last year's khaki leaves, nor do I feel sensations of birth at the onslaught of winter. We're out of sync, He and I. Add to that the communication issue: I don't think He notes, much less cares, if my Catholic husband eats a burger instead of branzino on Fridays, and I wonder what his timeline is on the forgiveness of sins. But for the grace of God, we don't fall into hellfire; but for the grace of God, the gossamer thread from which we dangle over burning coals does not tear.

On this year's day of resurrection a friend drops by to talk about her husband of thirty-one years. She learned two weeks ago that he, provider of Princeton educations and vacations in Barbados, of a stately Tudor and a Manhattan pied à terre, he, the ethical media man in cashmere, the stalwart head of family, had been unfaithful for more than a decade. Having moved out a week ago to assume his new (or alternate) life, he had Passover with *her* and *her* friends, and it was all very pleasant. His email said the food was good, the company so nice. "But," my friend demurs, "he says he missed the ritual of our Passovers. The ritual?" She stares at me and all I see are cerulean rings around pupils too big for my bright kitchen lights. "That's what he missed?" She re-crosses her fine legs and brushes back highlighted hair that fits her head like the cap of an acorn. He's not even Jewish.

The ritual, the spicy incense, that's what brought me back, unfaithful though I was, agnostic verging on atheist that I was even at sixteen. Who could resist on Christmas Eve, our bellies full of roast beef and Bordeaux, our ears full of Jingle Bells and Merry Men? Leaving the gravy to congeal on the plates, we'd pile into the Studebaker and rumble up the road to the Gothic stone church whose bells pealed with the promise of mystery, invisible velvety mystery that held us in its palms as my father glided through Stop signs in a stupor of alcohol. Late and unstable, in long dresses and black ties, my parents, my brother, and I would squeeze into a back pew as the priest in gold thread passed by swinging his thurible of hot coals and incense, and choir boys in red and white floated by with cherubic cheeks and mouths open in song, inspiring the faithful to stand, to sing, to hail the coming day. They processed beneath a gold cross up the nave to the chancel where candlelight echoed on stained glass and heady myrrh enfolded the hemlock and poinsettias. By the time of the sermon, my father's eyelids had fallen and his stertorous breathing braided the booming words of promise.

On the windowsill at home, among red Santas and reindeer, we had set up a wooden crèche. Mary in blue knelt in perpetuity, and Joseph stood with his staff nearby. Shepherds with skins tossed over their shoulders were approaching, a donkey was dozing, and cattle lay on their bellies. Bits of straw survived storage from year to year and filled the cradle where I placed the baby. My brother liked to perch him on the stable roof to gaze, I imagine, at the star of his birth though a Venetian blind blocked the view. After Christmas I never gave the crèche another look—not when we put away decorations each January, not when my father died and we went through the old house we had to sell. We threw out the whole brown box whose sides were collapsing, the hand-painted figures in this play of maternity and questionable paternity, the baby with his pudgy legs drawn up, his arms free of swaddling, his eyes too focused for an infant, too calm for a messiah, his size the breadth of my palm.

When the family dispersed, and I left home for good, there followed a stretch of fidelity to the flesh. Sex offered more tangible transcendence and more give and take than did a relationship with omniscience—and greedy omniscience at that. Not once had a hymn scoured the depths of the human heart, not once had a prayer turned up clues to the chaos of cancer or the hanging of men by their arms in frigid, hidden cells.

And then there were wars, always wars, that could not be resolved since everyone involved, as Dylan reminded us, had God on their side—a god who supplied purpose and drive and arms and reason and justification to die. Suicide bomber approaches the Kadhimia Shiite shrine in Baghdad yesterday, shouts "God is Great," and detonates a blast that kills sixty adults and children, including Iranian pilgrims who had come to pray. One man loses thirteen family members. A widow remarks, This morning we were happy. Whatever God is up to is cryptic to me, but millions assume they are privy to his plans. Back in 1805 a Seneca chief, Red Jacket, asked some insistent missionaries why, if God intended everyone to have the Bible, the Indians hadn't gotten copies.

God is remiss and quixotic (the kind that keeps one guessing) but excuses come easily for those we love. When I was a kid, Sunday school teachers told me that God was love and that He was everywhere, so I figured He didn't miss much. I imagined Him in the air, bumping against the arms of chairs, warming beneath the shade of my bedside lamp, battling the witch in my closet, freshening the pears in the refrigerator drawer. Not only was He everywhere, but He had *always* been everywhere. He never began. With love, we're more concerned with the end.

My friend's husband told her he was emotionally shut down and, yes, celibate. The veracity of the statement or lack of carries no more weight than dust on a windowsill, but the statement itself is grounds for divorce. Wanting to maintain the status quo, she turned the other cheek and was, covertly, relieved. She could deal with that. She could live side by side, greeting him coolly when he arrived home at 10:00 and said work was tough. Now that he's gone, she does not miss him, but she misses a body, a body to be sitting on the couch at 4 on a Saturday afternoon, a body to ride home with after a movie, a body to walk down the stairs after midnight and interrupt for a minute the clank of old pipes and sighing of rain on a shingle roof, a body to be with her at their son's wedding next month. She'd rather be married than not, but she'd rather not be married to him. I'd rather have religion than not. But true fidelity to one entails missing other visions of delicious uncertainty, like the castle on a cliff in Spain you see from the road and don't have time to stop for because it's not on the agenda or somebody has to piss. Oh, you think in dreamy consolation, I'll come back, knowing full well you won't.

In the meantime I confess to maintaining ritual. It's the closest I can come to reading the Jungian archetypes that I'm told are engraved in my psyche and yours—rituals that may be a second cousin once removed of those archetypes, born out of particular British Episcopal traditions with only a flicker of the sensation, a single cell of the lineage of those archetypes. That will suffice. In December I gather hemlock and holly from nearby woods and sit on the kitchen floor making wreathes, the only handicraft I learned from my nanny and the only one I have passed on to my children. On Christmas Eve I wear silk and pull the curtains, tuck balsam behind the pictures, and light red candles around the house. We call the ornaments shinies because my great uncle did, and we place the stockings at the end of the bed to be filled with things wrapped in red and green tissue because my mother did. From the house filled with carols arises a ghostly temptation to go to a midnight service, but I resist.

The other 364 days of the year we eat dinner together, more or less, and I inevitably burn the bread.

Perhaps if I'd had lower expectations of God, He'd still be around. Perhaps if my friend had been less exacting about her husband's tie, beard, mild flirtations, and time of arrival home from work, he would not have looked elsewhere, but who knows. In hindsight, having been raised on both resurrection myths and *Cinderella*, I don't know if I expected more from God than from a husband, but I do know that one has given me children and one has not. My friend's daughter, who is starting to look for marriage material, dismisses one guy after another. He wears a cross, she couldn't possibly look at that all day. He has a ying yang tattoo on his leg, what a turn-off. He buys turkey burgers instead of beef, wears his pants too short, plans vacations on the second date, burps, breathes. Meanwhile, my friend's choices shrink daily, a simple fact of demographics, of mortality. My god choices have withered too, through my own intolerance, but like my friend's husband who texts her every day to ask about assembling bookshelves and boiling tortellini, He hasn't gone away—not the memory of Him stretched across a night sky when the moon whispers light into an orchid of clouds, nor the chill when a B minor chord mushrooms in the dome of St. Peter's, nor the hint of order when I hang a wreath on my door.

The March of Days

A day, another day, the march of days, day in and day out, all day, a long day, every day and everyday days—we fling the phrases as perfunctorily as laundry into a sagging hamper. Days like a winter-thin leaf swept off a tree and tumbled under the porch, days cut short like a baby crab whose shell lies empty at the edge of the water, food for a gull that went on and ate another, days like a loaf of sliced bread, or a moist magnolia blossom, days in which a few minutes define the day because you only remember that piece like a slice of warm pear pie, a moment of birth, or a moment when you met your kid at the bus like any other day, or picked out Spectacular Speculoos ice cream at the supermarket. Who can pin it down, this thing, this airy non-thing called a day?

Blue days, yellow days, mauve, ochre, and sable. Holidays.

We must believe that the day has an inherent and universally understood quality of its own if we are to change it, just as I'd need to know the malleability of clay or obdurateness of marble before sculpting it. But what is it, that ill-defined, unsaid essence of day-ness?

What did I do last February 20? I couldn't tell you though on that day I was awake, conscious, sentient. Were it a weekday I know what I would have been doing, based on an external construct called a job. If a weekend, I see only a filmy blur of generic Saturday activities like reading the *Times* and standing in line at the dry cleaners. Seems wasteful, somehow, this incinerator of days filled with ashes and embers, sending a curlicue of smoke into a night and warming the anonymous hands of the homeless.

When I was seven or eight, I used to make movies on notepads, usually stick figures jumping off cliffs or popping balloons, sometimes a horse at a full gallop, each page advancing his strides with a shaggy mane flung back and tail streaming out behind. One page at a time.

Days spent or days in the mind are like flipping through those pages, speeding up the movie or halting it or missing it when pages stick or skip, days laboriously constructed, which after the fact only contribute instantaneously to a narrative that always ends before you want it to. Do you want to see it again? I'd ask a friend, who'd shrug and amble away because why would she?

Some days accommodate unanticipated stuff in large volume, making me believe I can stretch the day the way leggings yield generously to the belly after Thanksgiving dinner. Look! I managed to do this and this and this. Other days rip open like a flimsy plastic bag toting a single carton of grapefruit juice whose corner splits the seam in the parking lot just as you look away to open the trunk, leaving the bag useless, the juice an annoyance that you carry inside like an ignoble trophy. I imagine old age is increasingly that, the single task of bathing or making a scrambled egg, skillfully or ineptly executed.

But what sense are all these images of nature and instances of human foibles that only connote what a day is *like?* I'm like a lioness out to hunt who circles her target only to be duped when a competitor strikes the antelope unseen. I circle around the quality of a day, even stroke its back and divine a texture, but cannot look in its face and say ha! It is you! I've found you out at last.

Measurements and classifications prove useless. Knowing the sun will set at 4:24 today and 4:25 tomorrow says less than nothing about the flesh and blood of the day, its language, its smell—nor does it signify if I have affected the day as artfully as I would wish. Some means of measurement are significant in the cosmic placing of the globe in relation to the sun, I guess, but who thinks of that as they watch the clock tick away their lunch hour and hurry back to work, knowing the clock chops the day into cubes, ranging from the inedible to the delicious.

Sometimes waiting turns time into a smooth black highway, the kind out west that goes for hundreds of miles between towns and a child asks at odd undesignated intervals amidst field upon field of indifferent corn, Are we there yet? A friend of mine has a niece in Indiana whom he visits twice a year, in November and April. Somewhere around September eight-year-old Sabrina texts him, Is it *days* yet?

* * *

There's an assumption in America that everyone wants a "nice" day, or at least we tell others to have one. Nice is bland to begin with, I wouldn't want to be described that way; furthermore, we've worn the phrase so threadbare that I find myself grimacing to indicate the impossibility of such an outcome. The British suggest having a "good" day, or a "fine" one, while the French pare it down to simply *bonne journée,* or "good day," issued as tersely as *merci* to put an end to a conversation or transaction. Somehow it lacks the cloying diffidence of the American variation, and possibly the insincerity, though that's debatable, and sounds almost omniscient and affirmative. In recent years it seems the platitude has given way to the smiley emoticon, which at least leaves some ambiguity about who is having the nice day, the one sending the text or the one receiving it, a commentary on the subject of the text as it pertains to the sender or a wish from the sender that the recipient feel happy. It saves words. Just as the mouth issuing a heart saves us from the ubiquity of *I love you* in lieu of *goodbye.* And saving words saves time, of which a day is made. But is *have a nice day* truly an imperative? My boss would never say it though the CVS clerk might as I sign for shampoo. Or is it a wish, a subordinate clause following an understood "I hope that you…have a nice day." Am I in possession of the day already? Or does someone hope that I will and that it will treat me well? Or I will treat it well, cupping it in my palm like a pet hamster or a stone you pick up on the beach and think, for a silly minute or hour, you will keep.

My daughter's kindergarten teacher used to say, "Sophia arrives at the door each day lit up like a Christmas tree." She wore second-hand pink skirts and pushed her too-short bangs back with a plastic gold headband as if her bangs had grown out; she wore Mary Janes and for the sake of fashion refused all forms of sweaters. All this was pretty ordinary for a little girl trying not to be her big brother so that wasn't it. It was a matter of light and energy in her eyes and her missing-front teeth smile assuring her world that she was not going to miss a minute of block building or clambering up slides or spinning on tire swings or splashing primary colors on recycled paper and calling it a family portrait. I've known others who alter the light in a room. And the play of light, as a group of painters over a century ago realized, determines our perception in any given moment be it sun slanting over a bay, turning it molten silver, or dawn flinging the shadow of a peony, or white light bleaching the sand, or the studded spear of the Chrysler Building shrinking skyscrapers and dulling their quotidian glow. Remaining a detached observer in the presence of such people is a metaphysical impossibility, but I don't know if their sculpting of a day makes me any wiser or perspicacious, makes me see this thing, a given day, with more clarity due simply to change they usher in and I, by association, feel.

Sometimes I miss a day, totally miss it. Now the definition has nothing to do with time; it is synonymous with things that matter, like going for a run or seeing daylight before you go in to work or seeing it after. When I leave work in the dark I wonder if I've been asleep and dreamt what happened in the daylight I can only presume occurred, invisible daylight that hypothetically validated the mechanical or dreamy movement of the previous eight hours. Another day, another dollar becomes the most tangible if pedestrian definition of a particular span of time that deliberately eludes color, flavor, feel, lest such sensation deter us.

On the other hand, I remember looking down a hillside of terraced rice paddies in Bali and telling myself consciously, remember this day, remember the sun lighting spears of rice, spider-like shadows across the water, a white water buffalo knee deep, a man plucking shoots, scallop upon scallop of water, like so many harps lying down, tier upon tier on the side of a mountain whose crest was cradled by clouds. I would turn to go and then say to myself, turn around, look again, stamp it on your brain, and I tried. Now I know only what year that was; if I knew the month and day the numbers might be auspicious, or not.

My brother's lucky number when we grew up was 17, which seemed odd to me even back then. I always liked the even ones, especially 4. Two weeks after our mother died I fell on ice and shattered my wrist.

That day was December 17. Is there anything to say or think other than, ironic? 12/17. My father died on 12/12 while I was out buying a Christmas tree. The numbers connect like bulbs on a string of lights, one red, one blue. And whenever I buy a Christmas tree the day becomes 12/12.

My brother and I used to ask each other: if the house were burning down, what would you take? Definitely Peter Rabbit, Frederick Theodore, and Teddy (top three stuffed animals); the coin collection, my diary, his baseball cards. Now I'd say laptop, family photos, puppets from Bali, my father's war medals. When I'm about to die will I wonder what days to keep, what days I have kept…and why? Will the arrangement be as random as the things that take on meaning, as senseless to anyone other than me? Will the days spill like cataracts from a rock cleft, spitting and moiling on impact with a river below? Or will they be numbers, or images transfigured and frozen by time or memory, or a photo that conflates the two?

But no, nothing so palpable or familiar. I'm afraid the days will be bands of refracted light, sweeping strokes of gauzy oranges and reds in which no instant is individuated or concrete, and dawn no more gentle (as it is) than dusk.

If the house were burning, I'd want to choose, take my time, sit back and say, I'll take all the stuffed animals, not only three, take the day of my first memory (having my stomach pumped out in a hospital), the day I gave birth, the day I gave birth again when my body, at least, remembered the other time, take my son's broken tooth, my daughter's tears.

Bowl

When I emptied my mother's apartment, I meant to be decisive and steely, leaving her filmy cocktail glasses and Portuguese vases for Good Will under the gaze of two cast iron standing lamps, which also would be left behind like sentinels at an army base. I moved fast, wrapping china for my kids and their future apartments, tossing Glad Wrap, and abandoning *The Collected Stories of Eudora Welty* with scarcely a twinge. High on the urgency to dismantle, to undo, to get out of sight all those items she once polished and prized, I might have missed it—a metal bowl wedged behind a canister of Eukanuba. My nanny mixed Clorox and water in it with which to scrub my father's cuffs; my uncle's golden lab lapped water from it under my crib. Fifty years left patches of eczema and rusty eyes inside and out. Blindsided, I sat down and cupped it in my palms, feeling its gritty patches and skinny protruding lip, remembering its buttery yellow. Twice that night, with a furtive glance at the windowpanes, I fished it out of the trash.

Bowls rank high among artifacts in my attic or the back of kitchen cabinets. Tarnished as a pigeon, my mother's first porridge bowl lies wrapped in newspaper, a proper silver one with her initials engraved in the basin and a scalloped handle stemming from one side. Somewhere, awaiting excavation, is my son's first cereal bowl, sturdy like him, with Beatrix Potter bunnies figured in the center and leaves the color of key lime pie curling around the rim. My husband eats Wheat Chex from a bowl lifted from the Amherst cafeteria, circa 1976, depicting Lord Jeffrey Amherst on horseback chasing Indians in a perpetual circle around the rim, an image to trigger the appetite. From the pottery wheel of a college friend who studied in Japan came a stack of celadon cups with no handles, which stand largely neglected on my top kitchen shelf. I used to sit on the floor serving tea and feeling artsy, cupping the warm little bowl and thinking how simple, how useful, this bowl shape that crosses geographic and temporal borders. A containment of rice, a silent request on a stoop for quarters and dimes, a nest under an eave. Later I divined brilliance in my toddler placing balls in a bowl only to dump them out and repeat the drill.

On my blue and white bowls from Hanoi, dragonflies waft with undulating tails and taro plants spread their symmetrical leaves. The guidebook tells me the image is rustic and traditional. To me the limpid gray background and morning-blue lines that someone has drawn time and again are rare and beautiful. That is all I know but (with apologies to Keats) not all I need to know. Form is history, history form. I keep them high in a glass cabinet and refuse to put them in the dishwasher; their duplicates in Vietnam have been handed down, washed in rivers and buckets and sinks, till there remains, perhaps, a telltale wing. Like the Temple of Dendur sitting on Fifth Avenue where buses cough and vendors hawk African figures and Italian pashminas made in China, the bowls are involuntary stories, displaced and partially read.

I have a stoneware mixing bowl from my childhood, a wide brimmed bowl with a white ring like a lucky stone. Too big to keep in any kitchen cupboard, it sits in the cellar on top of an empty flowerpot. Gazing into its chipped basin, I feel like an oracle awaiting a sign in heady and potent fumes, but our futures are cloudy. Instead, I see myself standing on a kitchen chair, wooden spoon clenched in my small fists. Round and round, counter-clockwise, slow and deliberate, the muscles in my forearms aching, I ploughed the spoon through gluey dough, picking up granules of sugar and flour until all cohered while my mother anchored the bowl in her arms, a bowl that her mother (whom I never knew) brought from England. We only used it at Christmas to make cakes with nuts and rubbery bits of red and green fruit. And so is this bit of history circumscribed. And so will it go unseen by anyone who finds the bowl and its cargo of dust. This is vintage, they'll say, cool.

I'm busy getting and spending and already envisioning dispensing things before my kids have to pack my house, divide the goods, divine the ancestry, mock the out-datedness, and conflate my history with that of a tangerine bowl picked up on a back street of Pienza. I've inherited silver bowls, which I tuck in a cupboard, bearing initials I don't even know. When my son asks, I study the stylish loops, and the mystery seems momentarily grave. I gave him one this Christmas, 1916 engraved on the bottom below the name of the jeweler in the town where I grew up. Lingering on a sideboard is an ornate sugar bowl with round handles on two sides and a spoon whose neck curves like an S. The spoon itself is a shallow bowl with tiny holes through which I used to sprinkle snowdrifts of sugar onto inedible Shredded Wheat. It's defunct now. Sticky brown sugar, jagged natural sugar, whatever sugars my kids will allow their kids will never pass through.

The yellow bowl sits under my sink behind the dog biscuits and Comet. Its blotches resemble moon craters dug by an asteroid winging through the heavens, or the melanoma cut from my thigh twelve years ago. My bowl is useless, though. I'll dump it in the recycling bin but the absurd question is when.

Imagine

It's Chaddy's birthday today. She would've been 96.

I would've been checking the stove and turning off lights, running back inside to check again since I believe one day I will burn down my house. I would've wrapped another nightgown from L. L. Bean, taken a container of fresh applesauce for her from the freezer, scrambled for my glasses, heaved a sigh, loaded the CD player, and headed down the highway. I would've played music to make your blood run, music not to think. I would've taken the turns fast and close, ascending the GW Bridge and pumping across with as much matter-of-fact will as the truckers bearing down behind me. Again. Yes, I would've thought, again. I hadn't missed my mother's birthday since college when who knows where my head was. One year I made a cake and carried it on Amtrak from Manhattan to Phillie, changed to a local, and walked through three feet of snow to our house, cake laden and cold. I would've thought *me* again, my brother gets off easy living in Wisconsin. And it'll be me next year and the next because she's going to live to 100. We were so certain.

Passing Newark, Newark Airport, Elizabeth, East Brunswick, oil refineries and inverted pears of solid smoke, I would've remembered suddenly that I should have brought flowers, and I would've remembered the earthy smell of her chrysanthemums in pots on her terrace years ago, little yellow heads in the sun. I would've seen her stand up, brush back her hair with a hand caked in dirt, and fetch the hose to soak the pachysandra she just planted around our front door. The woman could work, the woman was compulsive. I would've thought, how could I forget. And she, who rarely goes outside. Winter now, no flowers.

I would've reached the Pennsylvania Turnpike and slowed the pace. Half hour or so to go. Two lanes and slow moms, kids in tow. Some of the adrenaline would filter away. Open fields on either side. I would've reached the exit for our old house and thought about taking it—maybe taking it—though staying on the highway ten miles farther would bring me closer to the nursing home faster. Yes, why not. I would've skimmed up and down the hills of Gulph Road, under dogwoods and oaks nearly unrecognizable in February, would've turned down the dead end street and groaned at the sight of the stone house she had cared for like a well-groomed child (when we were gone or out of reach), the glass room my father had built, amputated, and replaced by a two-story prefab white structure, nearly windowless, three garages appended to the side where there had been a stretch of lawn and a bank of ferns. I would've cried inside (for a second) at the Japanese maples that I used to climb, trees a friend of my grandmother brought as seedlings in a flowerpot from Japan circa 1920. I would've shrugged and told myself to steel myself because that's what you do (remembering the gently rippled bark), turned in a single smooth motion around the circle at the dead end, and headed to see her with renewed respect for what she had tended and lost. And would that have made me respect her more? Love more? Staring, that is, at the brazen futility of any of it.

I would've passed my old school, changed the music and wondered about Annie, Liz, lacrosse games, and eighth-grade parties. I would've tapped my foot at stoplights, regretting my detour, asking why I let myself go back. Masochist. Just get there. Have the birthday. She'll be asleep anyway, she'll fall asleep again anyway. In a day she won't remember I came, anyway.

Or maybe I would've stayed on the highway. Never hopscotched back in time. Called my daughter. Listened. Planned the weekend ahead. With the boyfriend, yes, of course. Arrived with my mind on auto-fill.

Pulling into the Quadrangle driveway, I would've sighed, stiffened. Ahead, the two-story brick apartments and clean sidewalks, the absurd mini-speed bumps slowing already comatose cars for no one. I would've opened my door, been startled by the cold, shivered slightly as I reached for the gift and the just thawing applesauce. I would've walked like a sleepwalker under the awning, through the large door, into the elevator with its oversize green and red buttons and oversize numbers, found her asleep in the hallway waiting to go in or out of a meal. And I would've greeted her as if she were home in the big house and I, just arrived, "Happy Birthday, Mom!" and she all smiles for a minute, she with the ruddy complexion year round and red lipstick and white hair still permed. Even now she would've smiled for an instant, scrunching her little brown eyes, and I'd imagine that for a split second maybe she felt something run through her veins, something like life, like happiness. And then I'd wheel her to her room and I would've talked while that feeling passed and she slept away the moments she used to find precious, the moments I was there.

I would've stayed while she slept, checked my email impatiently and frequently. I would've woken her from time to time to feed her applesauce and hear her say it's wonderful, and enjoy the infrequent smile. I would've remembered the applesauce she used to make for me, year in, year out.

I would've resisted knowing that she knew I'd soon be gone. That's just the way it was.

Left Unhung

In a museum to see four-year-olds touching Da Vincis. Couples nearly making out. Black sneakers and rude bodies moving like slow fish between me and the art, distorting, altering the shot pheasant on a table with movement of bodies absorbing the pheasant, momentarily, unless they pause to take a picture of the picture to look at it in their kitchen or not at all, a dead image in a phone, testament to them. French everywhere. I stand before a clear crisp painting of a brown and white jug on a brown and white table. Flat linear, it's all about straight lines and where they intersect with diagonal ones and how the diagonal ones parallel each other. It's all about that, meaning what? Why a sudden interest in the angle that a jug makes with a table? What perspective when I place a pitcher of maple syrup on the table, and sticky rings gaze heavenward. Strollers plod like mules, flung jackets, toddlers at the breast. Dark Dream, disguised elephant, broad leaves. Tail-lit lion. Moon, white moon, marble moon. Nude on a sofa in the jungle. Clearly, Rousseau never left France. I'm three times removed. So why is this pleasing? Is it pleasing? My dreams aren't in color. Now I see blurry images of pines growing out of rocks by Cézanne. Yes, the colors are pleasant (earthy ochres and reds and turquoisy blues) ... do I feel affirmed that another eye sees trees smudge, rocks stand at attention, branches cry? Is that why? Suppose I'm off kilter, out of whack, mortality skewing my city till it blurs, brilliant street light supercedes car light supercedes trash bin on the corner, guy selling pashminas for $3. I always went to museums to see pictures I knew from books, to recall words constructing context and describing painterly qualities, the interplay of light and life, to think I know that, it's familiar, familiar odalisque on a duvet naked and rosy a full century or two ago so was it about me or her? Sad

Picasso eyes head on, the girl braiding her hair, all triangles, triangular chin, triangular vulva, rope of hair over her shoulders, but form be damned, it's those sad head-on eyes. Same eyes in the three women from Avignon, straight on, but blank and empty way past sad. Whip through social realism...all thick army green and garish. Woman's torso tied up, very subtle, guy sitting by pigs on a farm in Anywhere, America. On to the clean Mozarty world of Mondrian. I had a dress like that, crisp red line intersects with yellow square, intersects with thicker blue square. No confrontation, just gentle crossings, and plenty of white space in between. Not New York. Space, cleanliness, order, idea. But I move on not knowing exactly what that is. Like jazz. My husband always gets the form. But it's out there gyrating in space just asking, begging to be translated into I'm a lonely bum or I'm about to come and can't wait another second or the world is too ineffable, I just can't tell you. And the gypsy dreaming feet sticking up, flute slippering around his head, everywhere smooth round lines and moonlight and a lion licking in your ear, telling you of dark tree roots and ribs and prides and not hungry... Van Gogh's swirling café at night looks like too many posters of same, sickly suspicious skin eyes askance under your straw hair—were you really crazy or was that a stunt after your mom used your paintings as fuel? Gio wafts from old men. Artists with names like pasta, Severini, Broccoli, I don't know you, you don't move me, I move on to an undisguised room full of photos where a gaggle of middle school girls giggles at the naked black man with shiny shoulders, the naked plump girl beside her fully clothed mother, the contortionist in tight jeans her back bent, legs splayed, head coming between her knees. Tiny black and whites, could be my dad on horseback in Montana in 1921 when he had polio and was sent out west for health, could be my dad watching Lindbergh's plane land outside Paris after the first trans-Atlantic flight...too small now, I'm impatient...stunning blue white apricot, woman head flung back in cloudy white, floating in what she feels, that head thrown back, and beside it in the shadows of trees face hidden by shadows a boy or girl I can't tell holds a sheet of paper and lights it on fire, fire licks up the page, but the page is still white, something still legible on her side, his side, not mine, what black words turning blacker, charred smudged, I can't see can only imagine, like Antigone when a messenger recounts the battle that killed her brother and left his carrion body in the dust, she cannot see him, only a negative of a picture a messenger creates and leaves unhung. Always the state of burning, always the state of being eaten, of turning to smoke. Around the corner, a line of models in designer shades, how implacable and chiseled, red political pamphlets all balled strewn across the floor denouncing Tito, suddenly art. Women in media, women abused, male conceived, framed and sold. In this morning's paper: Somali girl buried to her neck and stoned for saying no to Shabab commander. Gang rape as political gesture. Pretty victim covers her face, covers her eyes with her hands in shame, blue chador over her head and shoulders, early morning blue, blue memory of Vermeer's girl with a white pitcher before a sunlit window, white face in the sunlight, Somali in my recycling bin in the garage. Photo glass and frames gleam like so many knockoff Rolexes. On to the great Metaphysical Interior. Meta-art, meta-spectator, meta-painting, a lesser known one, the wiry blonde in Prada shades and bunny fur nudges past, but wait, there's an easel in the picture, a three-story building, fountain, ripply mountains all complete, a tease or an excuse, still propped inviting the painter's invisible hand, and beside it could that be bread, a painting of a painting of baguettes? The café will be jammed. De Chirico's train stands frozen in departure, smoke pluming upright like a soldier at attention, plume erect in a simultaneous world of vagary wind streaking taut (fap-fap-fap) the banners over Gare Montparnasse. Buy postcards of favorites, get the express.

Tennis: *Fort-da!*

There was an unopened can of balls. With a touch of your finger, as God's to Adam's, and a gentle tug, you unleash virgin air with a whoosh. Into your palm drop three worlds, yellow as the warmth of new suns, round enough to spin through heavens, mapped like ancient Pangaeas. You will move continents.

FORT-DA!

(GONE-THERE!)

—SIGMUND FREUD

Suddenly, without explication, one is lost. *Fort!* Damn! It's not caught in the metal fence, nor tucked in the first weeds of spring. You don't believe it has rolled to the adjacent court and yet you wander there and trace the line where horizontal Har-tru and vertical fence meet. You fling your eyes heavenward in hopeless disbelief, wondering if the ball flew over the fence when you were dashing unaware, or if your partner purposely angled a shot as Freud's little grandson hurled objects out of sight again and again. What is loss? You are desire incarnate, just wanting that ball—be it a substitute for your forever lost mother or not.

Da! As if reeled in by a string, it has rolled back to the overturned can to resume a safe existence before conscious life. There is no joy in recovery without absence, no win without loss. You cannot let it rest or there will be no story.

131

JUDGMENT
ANGELS AND PEDESTRIANS

You have time to turn your hips, hear the rough scruff of your sneakers, rotate the shoulder, flatten your wrist, whack the ball at hip height as the racket head picks up speed, hear the effortless ping, swing through and feel it grace your opposite shoulder as you smugly watch the sexy arc cross court into the depths of the forehand corner, power thrilling through your capillaries, as the ball falls somewhere deep in a shadow where the baseline intersects with the inside alley line in a neat ninety-degree corner within a crisp two-inch hem. No racket touches that ball. For a moment you feel its precision like the first prick of a tattoo needle. But your opponent raises one hand and points with certain nonchalance. Was all that grace and power a lie? A mirage of incandescent angels fluttering over cornices of monolithic stone? You want to see, knowing you don't need to see. You want the ease and surge again—it's in your blood like a drug. You're not convinced in your soul the ball exceeded legitimate space though you have to believe your partner or concede to him at the very least, but even though it went out it was in—in a sense—if your life is defined by form and beauty. There will be no discussion, you're too poised to contest a point. Still, with his back to you and with a flick of the index finger, a moment of fluid connectivity has been rendered null and void. Do you dare that shot again, shaving some power off the swing, tilting the racket head more sharply like the cocked head of a cobra? Or do you take the racket back only half as far, swing, connect, stop the racket as it reaches the anticipated direction of the ball, feel the sink of dull concession inside as it leapfrogs over the net in slow motion, airy and loopy? It's in. Play continues, but your shallow shot leaves you vulnerable; you watch his body language the way you note a man's when he turns the key in the lock and walks in the door at the end of the day with a sigh. There is that much time. You sidestep uneasily. Will he seize the chance to put the ball down your throat or send you a handsome backhand and keep the rally going for the sake of a good aerobic workout, a pleasant waltz as one's mind drifts to champagne and canapés? You marry the latter and dream of the former. Now you're playing his game, not yours. Reconsider criteria. Rewind and judge your first shot. Can you call it good?

TORTS AND DISCLAIMERS

I flail at the ball and hit it catastrophically into the net, with a wail, "Did you see that bounce?" Clearly, a nick in the court or a pile of Har-tru sabotaged what would have been a sizzling return.

Recently I heard a story of a guy who broke into a house through a skylight. Because the window was faulty he fell and broke his leg. The would-be burglar filed a claim and got some money. By law one thing has nothing to do with the other.

Not so on this court: the game *is* the ripple where the tape protrudes and I can catch my toe. It *is* the gusts that spiral my toss and buoy my lob two inches farther than planned. This game entertains no excuses, nor are the white lines the only parameters I need to measure.

I know a woman who broke her ankle on a flight of stairs because the light was out, though she knew the light was out and chose to take the stairs. She filed a claim because the building was wrong and she was right, and whether she initially believed it or not, she came to believe it was true.

THE EFFECT CANNOT BE MORE PERFECT THAN THE CAUSE.
—RENÉ DESCARTES

Return a serve at a 20-degree angle to the net with a kiss of your racket, and watch it ease into the next court like a child skipping from home at dusk, and your gentle move will seem greater than the serve that you assumed to be the cause due to its ontological position and higher speed.

You think it's over. You think on this Cartesian court and by thinking establish your existence, which is very wrapped up in your validity as winner of the point. Your spirit soars, your body, the lesser entity, fails to register your opponent's move, making all too tangible the disastrous effects of the dichotomy. It was only the plan of an orderly god, say some followers of Descartes, (I'd call it chance) that ever gave us the notion the two acted in sync. Imagine mind and body as two clocks, both wound by Him. When one reaches two o'clock, the other chimes, giving an illusion of connection, even causality, when in fact there is none at all. In the shadow of your delusional success (a clock that has virtually stopped), your opponent moves with elfish agility, scoops his racket under the ball, and sends it happily, unspectacularly, over the net in a second or two. Has he outdone the cause? Has he emasculated your deft caress? Left it as impotent as the word of god devolved into cliché?

Hume (playing Descartes) would claim there was no causal connection to begin with, no logical reason to believe that the opponent accomplished his shot because of the angle of yours, no logical reason to believe that an orange will taste like an orange rather than a chunk of pork other than the fact that by frequent association you come to expect the orange will taste like an orange. My slice was unexpected and uncharacteristic, impossible to anticipate by habit or association.

And imagine: between my will to slice the ball and any subsequent movement lies a sequence of intermediaries—nerves shooting wordless signals and hexagonal bundles of myofibrils grabbing one another to create bridges to release calcium ions, triggering my arm and leg and back muscles to contract, with the iambic meter of my heart accelerating on its own without the slightest request by my will—from which I can nearly deduce the presence of a muse and mystical things unseen by any human eye, so what a fool am I to infer a cause from an end. Advantage, Hume. From observation we learn nothing!

BETWEEN THE IDEA
AND THE REALITY...
BETWEEN THE CONCEPTION
AND THE CREATION...
FALLS THE SHADOW
—T. S. ELIOT, "THE HOLLOW MEN"

With a winning vision, I hit the ball flat down the line to the side of the court where he is not, and the ball balances momentarily on the highest part of the net like Nureyev on pointe only to fall on my side with oblivious innocence.

And I'm down a set.

THE I IS ALWAYS IN THE FIELD OF THE OTHER.
—JACQUES LACAN

In the instant when a ball flies toward you at 80 miles an hour, or a piece of toast burns, or a guy proposes, you don't have such time as did those old philosophers to reflect, project, object. You're not aware of thought as the primordial swamp from which the I arises, slick and slimy, to affirm its existence on dry land without prior experience in anything but ooze. Just as a baby can clench her fist before she can recognize herself in a mirror, so I can hit the ball without differentiating myself from my opponent's high toss, his arm cocked back, the ball growing brighter as it spears toward me in a descending ray, whisking over the net and bouncing as I sidestep, rotate my shoulder, hear a ping and watch the ball spin green to yellow in a diaphanous orb of sunlight until it drops perhaps nowhere near the spot I intended—and now he sets up with rapid little steps and a glance fired at me, our positions and the pathways of our shots drawing a pattern that is new only in its minor variations from patterns drawn by other players at other times. Hitting connects me to an encompassing other,

135

which is neither immortal nor divine. It is locus, Autre, the crisp rectangular court and the language of boundaries, speed, anticipation, and execution.

Nailing the ball back at me is my own projection (little autre), whose will and sidesteps and two-handed backhands bleed into mine as I decide whether to whip it down the line or cross court, hit with topspin or back spin, lob or slice. I swing and gaze after the ball as it advances on his field of vision and he sets up for an inside-out forehand that drops with bathetic malaise at the net, from which I judge not his shot but mine just as he replays my shot in the judgment of his. For a moment we have sifted the million mismatched reflections in the eyes of others (of which we are composed): only ours count.

He serves, sprints to net and volleys my lame return precisely where I am not, ending the point with the same blunt finality with which my thirteen-year-old true love walked away. I stare at him in disbelief, imagining another who never expected my short return, who never moved to net, who left me winning the point and feeling a jolt of power rather than cringing at my clumsiness. I'm nearly convinced the difference is as arbitrary as a judge's word without rule of law when I slam the truth down the center line of denial in my mind; one situation happened, the other did not. I handed him the shot like a breaded chicken cutlet on a china plate.

Yet, in the middle of the night, I wake up playing another game as if I were replacing the first, and the blue court of my mind becomes insatiable, parched desire to articulate what I never had the time or skill or wit to say. These are the vital battles, the invisible ones that connect me to another that is I.

Abruptly, the waking world sees something else: post-match I alight at the front door, breathless and smiling, placing my Wilson bag primly in view, or I shuffle in, shoulders flagging, shove the bag in the closet and retreat to the shower before braving the kitchen for a glass of water and the eyes, especially my mother's, that ask, well, did you win? What was the score?

EVE WITHOUT ADAM

Long before the language of scoring and all the complex choices of
adulthood—investing and risk taking vs. tucking away money in a
bank account that earns 1%, the rabid charge to net vs. the long gentle wait at the baseline for the lob to land—long before this there was
a backboard, half a court, no reflection, no other. Just me trailing
down a dirt road, stopping on a dam to chuck rocks and see them
hurtle to the river below. If I leapt could I clear the cement incline
and land in the water rearing up—the dark tobacco bubbles boiling
below? No, I couldn't, wouldn't, but I could never pull myself away
from picturing it. On I went along a ferny path with mud pocked
with the split hearts of deer hooves and the plaintive fingertips of
raccoons. Dew snuck through the toes of my Keds. No one was ever
there at that hour, not on the court nor in the wire cage housing two
backboards, divided by a fence running half the length of each space.
Clumps of grass stuck up here and there at the base of the wall and
fence poles, and the red clay surface dipped and rose like a gusty river.
A span of chicken wire some three feet high was strung along the top
of the wall, and if you launched the ball with enough verve, it might
catch there, suddenly immobilized, quickly a relic of a forehand gone
wrong. Sometimes I'd climb up the fence and reach, my arm extended by my racket, and try to gouge the wire and make the ball fall.
Sometimes another's ball would tumble instead, a ball that had been
soaked and dried till its fuzz wore down and rubber shell cracked. I'd
hit again and again, forehands, backhands, again and again. I don't
recall serving and there was no rushing to net. It was the essence of
playing myself. I could whack the ball with all the muscle power of my
eight-year-old arms, upping the tempo at will and paying, or slow it
down with a blooper placed to come back just where I stood and flick
it again as I listened to white-throated sparrows propelling their two-
pitched calls against the tips of hemlocks and beyond. Aside from spiraling the ball clear of the fence and losing it in the ferns, it was hard

to miss since the net was a line of paint and low balls that didn't clear it still came back. That was reassuring. Illusory. In line with the promises of potential we American children were taught. But my mind was not entertaining US Open trophies but flowing simply in my arm as it swung through with a desire to hit ever harder and smack the wall mere inches above that line. These hours laid the foundation of my game. I grew up to be labeled the human backboard, which I didn't find flattering in the least. It's a compliment, they claimed, but I knew better. Post Gloria Steinem, we recognized what objectification meant. And how ironic. With my boyish shorts and cropped hair, I had been the only player.

ENTER APOLLO AND DIONYSUS

Mr. Talbott had limbs like wisteria vines, gray eyes like a lake at dawn, a long lanky torso, and a protruding nose that was always redder than the rest of his face. He spent his days in the sun and his road map skin told the tale. He was calm and old fashioned. You simply had to shake his hand and he'd say, there's your forehand grip. He taught me to rotate my hand quickly counter clockwise to hit a backhand, take the racket back, watch the ball, swing and end with a graceful, suspended sweep, which would guide the ball to the desired point. Therein lay the principles of his game. I learned before the continental grip intervened between the other two, before the two-handed backhand came into vogue, and before anyone invented the now utterly indispensable topspin. No one served 140 miles per hour, and no one wrapped the racket clear around her head. I had a Chris Evert wood racket (with her autograph on the closed throat), which I put away each night in a trapezoidal frame with four screws. Otherwise it would warp in the damp mountain night, and all precision would be lost.

Decades later in the heat of a match, down a set and on the verge of trembling mental meltdown, I hear Mr. Talbott's voice and see his swing as a long, pure and continuous line that absorbs the frenzy of choice. I pause (Sharapova style, turning my back to my opponent for precisely counted, precious seconds) seeing my own physique as a smaller model of his, like an imitation statue of David sold in a Florentine gift shop. Form is preeminent. Maintain form and all else will follow. And so as the next ball approaches I concentrate on that alone, moving my feet, eye ever on the ball. The forces in the universe converge, mind and body line up like identical twins, and my return is elegant; the geometry works, and I feel a studied satisfaction. The very next shot I have only to duplicate the former...it smacks the tape at the top of the net, tumbling to my side miserably and inexplicably, taunting me with an eighth of an inch difference between success and failure.

It's mid-August in New York and I'm in the midday sun with a partner whose tennis passion runs like liquid iron at the earth's core; he's faster, fitter, younger than I, and he slugs the ball at me. My shirt clings to my abdomen, my palm slips, the top of my head tingles. Humidity as dense as the skies over Beijing leaves sweat trickling down the backs of my legs. I've lost track of the hours we've been out here, and in any given game, the score eludes me, the points are that long, my mind swept up in speed, heartbeat, anticipation, adrenaline, power, risk, the potential for precision or chaos. My racket decides and performs and the ball dances a dance that is choreographed and lost at precisely the same time. We play whole notes and staccato sixteenths. We calculate and move without calculation; we enact practiced form and concede its necessity by eradicating it as learned. We gulp water and switch courts without a glance or a word to break the spell.

From the sidelines my other world watches like Pentheus peering through the bushes, aghast at the maenads performing their ancient rites in the amber flush of the moon.

HEAVENWARD

To toss is as casual as flipping a coin, or chucking an old sock, or coating some lettuce leaves with dressing and giving them a good lift with wooden spoons. On the court one speaks of *the* toss. Introspective modes may warrant *my* toss, or didactic ones, *your* toss. But as you set up out there, planting your feet and tucking the backup ball in your pocket, you're thinking *control*. The toss has power, its own life, its own will; when you're edgy, it will take advantage . It may gyrate wildly in front of you with grave consequences that you foresee but elect to ignore as you dive in a moment of pure momentum, a schizoid moment when an ace assumes potent reality and the lousy toss guarantees a fault. You swing because your odds are low. Human perversity takes many forms.

Sometimes I cheat. I toss the ball wide to create a sharp angle to the serve when I should achieve that angle with my racket, or the direction of the swing, I'm never sure. It's not cheating per se but falling short of ideal form, a corruption of sorts, like *c u tonite*. Were the ball to drop on the ground, it should land on the head of a racket extending from and parallel to your front foot. Like getting pregnant, it can be harder than it sounds. Or not. I practice in the office.

I have to compose myself and concentrate. I slow my breathing and decide to think of something stationary. I always think of my mother in her wheelchair sitting from one meal to the next with her chin nodding against her rose cardigan. It's a solitary place inside my head, and hers.

ACT AS IF THE MAXIM OF OUR ACTION WERE TO BECOME
THROUGH YOUR WILL A GENERAL NATURAL LAW.
—IMMANUEL KANT

As well as you know him, his voice, the sound of his sleeping, the form of his topspin forehand, you know nothing (besides an intimation of *autre*) of those things themselves. You know them by sensations elicited by the experience of his voice, the sound of his sleeping, the form of his forehand. They exist in the time and space of your perception, the meshing of prior and present perception. You know his timing, his dance across a court, his pacing down a hallway, the timbre of his voice because it exists in the folds of your mind, heaped like a pile of clothes without logical order or sequence. Simply, you have worn them before. But sometimes you leap for a volley, turn the racket just so for a shot down the line, and you don't know where it came from.

140

You have not done it before, may not do it again; it was not learned from experience or evolved from observation. It happens intuitively and must come from your intuitive sense of time and space and way of viewing anything. In your shot lies the crux of Kant's persistent problem—how can a judgment be at once based on experience and already exist, a priori, independent of experience—the solution to which took him twelve years to figure out. No one has that kind of time.

Within the crisp perimeter of the court and the peculiar scoring of love, 15, 30, 40, and rules about net shots and foot faults, lie freedom and choice, however confined. Free will we must have, or all talk of strategy is drivel just as freedom must exist, says Kant, if there is such a thing as virtue. And with freedom come imperative decisions. You must say the ball is out, though you lose the point. You must say the ball you're unsure about is out, though you lose the point. You may choose to hit the most beautiful forehand that rises like a white crane lifting off a bay, a shot whose flight from the sweet spot of your racket elicits shivers as does a certain chord or turn of phrase, and on it sails, picking up speed as it plunges toward his baseline, though you hit it right to him and set him up for a winner.

THE DECLINE OF CIVILIZATION

You call his ball out. He questions your call. You smile calmly. He says let's take it over.

IMAGINARY TENNIS

Sometimes the ball goes out and he hits it anyway to keep it in play because a body in motion stays in motion. Or he felt like it. We continue with the fervor of a real point, knowing it was already over moments ago. Boom! Wham! Higher risks that are not risks. We're watching ourselves like a cartoon, wishing it were always that way.

141

BOLD LOVER, NEVER, NEVER CANST THOU KISS,
THOUGH WINNING NEAR THE GOAL—YET, DO NOT GRIEVE;
SHE CANNOT FADE, THOUGH THOU HAST NOT THY BLISS,
FOR EVER WILT THOU LOVE, AND SHE BE FAIR!
—JOHN KEATS, "ODE ON A GRECIAN URN"

Ah! the immortality of possibility, the timelessness of caught, immobile beauty, and the infinitude of love flush to the rim with desire that will never be anything else!

I launch myself toward a ball struck with breathtaking skill and hopelessly out of reach, a ball I never imagine touching while seeing it happen, seeing the place where the ball instantaneously will be and likely pass me by, sprint without hope and with visions of hope, a cell in some arterial current where movement (and not a moment caught in time) is timeless, stretching my arm, racket extending, insisting.

After the game I sit on a rock by the Hudson in a strong northerly wind. To my left a train bustles south toward the city, the red eyes of its tail lights narrowing as it moves away. To my right, out of earshot, a cargo ship also slides south, more slowly than the train, its wake widening behind. I remember throwing tennis balls at my kids, see them taking lessons on the same red courts where Mr. Talbott drilled my backhand, recall how they, too, tossed their racket into closets for years at a time, distracted and rebellious. For years my Chris Evert languished in the basement while Wilson produced aluminum ones in bubblegum pink, followed relatively quickly by graphite and graphite composites of titanium, kevlar, and fiberglass. When I resurfaced, I was quite the anachronism with my old racket, my cotton shorts and T-shirts, my terrycloth headband instead of a sweat-whisking Nike cap and spandex top with built-in bra. Now I've bought those things, added zest to my game! My children have been to Alaska and dyed their hair blue and dyed it back, been places I'm ignorant of and survived, dreamt dreams still furled like tight-fisted hyacinths in

March, found new places to live, new rackets to buy, and returned to the game. *Fort-da!*

TENNIS AND NOTHINGNESS

A hurricane has blown the Har-tru from the courts. Stripped sleek, they gleam in the four o'clock February sun, wettest in the middle, slightly paler around the perimeter of the doubles court. They sink in the middle too, as if they had exhaled and failed to take another breath, chest depressed, lungs at their last. Crusty ice laces the fence and a shadow lies where the white tape once marched in order. It will be months before a new sprinkling of green grit, months before the rolling and taping, and even then this process will depend on budgets and the vagaries of weather. There is no telling of time; scores are forgotten. The surface is as slick as a swamp and only squirrel tracks dance and dot the surface, relaying a very different game. A plastic A & P bag flaps crucified on the fence. It has no more meaning as a conveyer of groceries than does my racket as a conduit of being. No partner to call, no place to play. The word itself slinks away from the court and into a closet where I stare at it senselessly and it never flinches. Tennis tennis tennis tennis tennis tennis tennis tennis tennis tennis tennis tennis tennis tennis − my tongue welds the word into nonsense, the click of a hammer that accomplishes nothing and could stop anywhere or not at all. The fact that tennis could define me is true; the fact that absence of tennis could define me is true. Here I've slipped the confines of play, lost recognition of the racket, forgotten the feel of the innate possibility in a ball and the defining character of my forehand. I'm trying to appreciate the sensation of the nothingness of my practical identity—wait—is it death or freedom? And of what use, this freedom? *Da-Fort.*

30-40, DEUCE, AD-IN, DEUCE, AD–OUT, DEUCE, AD-IN, DEUCE, AD-OUT

We keep score. When it's deuce, it never simply is. Some advantage preceded and another will succeed.

HEARTSTRINGS

I wore leggings and an old sweatshirt that pulled under my arm when I served. Slowly I began to sweat under three layers, and I shed one to allow the easterly wind to nudge through fabric not intended for sports. Three o'clock and the sun sat like a cold ruffled sparrow in the limbs of a horse chestnut tree, which months before had dropped its lethal conkers underfoot. He served and the ball shot into a wind-designed pyramid of leaves in a corner of the fence. I pulled the ball from the sodden pile and bounced it quickly to dry. The sun caught his cheek for an instant before succumbing to a hull of advancing clouds. I remembered a day in August when boulders of bruised clouds had suddenly rolled in, sending all sensible players home. He leapt for an overhead, and as his racket stretched vertically and struck, a staggering branch of lightning shot down behind him cracking and hissing and soldering the line of his racket on my retina with the vertical reach of light.

Out of the corner of my eye, I saw two guys in wool coats and gloves release a gear on the net post of the farthest court, and the dance of strings gave way. They went methodically from one to the next, deflating each court and leaving us to play into the gloaming until they arrived with a tractor full of bundled nets, shovels, rakes, and scythes.

IV

How Could That Matter Now?

Twelve days after my mother died, I walked up my snow-dusted driveway, saw my boot slip back on black ice and pitched forward full force on one wrist. Hot wires shot up my arm. A bone shoved toward the skin's surface, my watchband strangled the skin above the bone. I held that arm like roadkill as I clambered up the hill to the house.

My husband drove me to the hospital, inching up the Saw Mill Parkway at 45. Ice, he said. We don't want to have an accident. Go faster, fuck it, go faster. Breaths stuttered shallow and spasmodic, faster. My hand veered to the side of my forearm at a 90-degree angle, and my arm was a tunnel in which lit nerves caught like fish hooks. Sweat seeped through my sweater. How do people wait for meds, people I read about every day, blasted by bullets, shrapnel, grenades? Then my fingers locked. Bent at the first joint, white as bone.

My stomach hiccupped as warm fluid rippled over the crags inside my hand. Lowered the volume, rounded the nail heads, and cloaked the embers. I breathed in. I was telling the nurse my mom just died. I was telling her I'd had two kids drug free and *that* pain hadn't come close. Just breathe, she said, clipping oxygen to my nose. I stiffened my legs under the sheet, saw my fingers move.

They kept the morphine coming (I assured them, pain level 8 out of 10) and a sexy Italian orthopedist with a chilly bedside manner showed up four hours later. It's bad, he stated, addressing my x-rays. Compound fracture, clear through the ulna and radius. He would reset it, but the splintered pieces might not stay, might slip. He'd have to re-x-ray, maybe put plates and screws in there in a few days when the swelling went down. For now, he wedged off my wedding rings, firmly embedded in my finger; then his cool hands took hold, pulled,

pulled again, rotated the arm, and realigned my bones. You have good hands, I said.

The last time I saw my mother, she wore a full-face oxygen mask. Her eyes were already closed, her cheeks still ruddy. She couldn't speak or had nothing to say. A morsel of food had slipped down the wrong way and landed in her lungs, blossoming into infection that coursed through her system. I sat on her bed, stroking her shoulder and tucking a blanket around her feet. I told her things I had never said and perhaps didn't quite believe, but how could that matter now? I read her a Sherlock Holmes story, as if sentences would bring coherence, even normalcy, but the syntax cracked and the words zigzagged like flies. Her right arm lay across her chest, fleshy and thick, her hand mottled with liver spots. She'd had a blood clot years ago and the arm had remained swollen, so she never wore short sleeves again.

I returned to work the next day, though I don't know why. While teaching a class of high school seniors, I glanced frequently at my phone. Between the files in my briefcase, a dull blue light flickered, and I stepped out of the room. She passed, a woman said, ten minutes ago. I caught my breath, held my breath. Turned 180 degrees and picked up the discussion of Carver's "My Father's Life." Did the essay convey more about the writer or his alcoholic father? Was the burst of sentiment at the end credible? I soldiered through the next day, teaching, meeting, answering questions from the crematorium, and trying to congeal my mother's life in a death notice of 100 words. No one at school needed to know.

I told close friends what had happened and how and when and yes, they knew she was very old, but the finality was hard. That was the party line, and you could say it as easily as fine, thanks, and you?

But a leaden vapor lurked in my mind like hot humidity before a storm, like smoke caught inside a warehouse fire, compelling me to resurrect not the old lady whose life was reduced to mushy food but the one who gave birth, ran meetings for nearly every music institution in Philadelphia, maintained her Main Line house at standards I used to ridicule, loved me enough to elicit feelings that I would never do enough, for her.

148

In the days following her death dense fog settled over the Hudson River where I live just north of Manhattan. The city lights blurred and receded, burning dully through early dusk like tarnished pearls. Such blatant objective correlative—but this wasn't fiction, this was life. As I walked past Riverview mansions and '70s split levels, I remembered her barrel laughter, the shape of her thighs and the snaps on her girdle with which she clasped the tops of her nylons before the advent of pantyhose. I remembered the marigolds in a silver bowl on her dining room table and my surprise that she let my three-year-old daughter pick them from her garden. I remembered how she kept my wild husky that I brought back from Alaska when I was eighteen and springing free from the strictures of private school and her, a dog too wild to go to college with me, though I tried. Maybe she figured giving the dog away would be tantamount to giving me away, so she kept her. That svelte wolf creature was powerful ammunition.

After the fog ebbed, my mother commandeered the snow. Wet clumps tumbled from the sky and schools closed for the day. Instead of teaching Dickinson, I sifted through photos of Chaddy and her two brothers with their austere nanny in England, photos of her holding my children, picnicking streamside in the Pocono Mountains, laughing skeptically at my father, walking her West Highland terriers through the campus of Bryn Mawr College where she had gone and her mother before her. Through the snow she moved in still lives with more grace than I had witnessed before when my own life punctuated hers with dashes and ellipses, and sentence fragments were left dangling like a questioning hand on a fractured wrist. I watched Dickinson's "certain slant of light" filtering under a flank of clouds and trembling across the icy river. The poet said that light brought "internal difference/ Where the meanings are" and I realized that I, and perhaps she, had only dug through drifts to the locus of meaning but not found one at all.

So, my mother didn't let go. On the day I would teach again I lay in the ER on morphine reminding myself she would not call; she would not bring me aspirin or sit by my bed. Mom, I fell. Dear Lord. When

I was three and kids still got mumps, she moved out of her bedroom to sleep with me on a fold-out couch in the playroom. And she didn't catch it. She was strong that way. She brought me bread and butter at night to help me sleep.

Casts are heavier than they look. At night if I dared roll over, I'd stop to deliberate on the placement of the supporting pillow. I sidled my body into position, then picked up the estranged arm, transferred it across my chest, and placed it like a china vase on the pillow, never knowing what minor lateral movement might jump start the nerve endings inside. With each shift I was fully cognizant, fully awake.

She created yawning chasms, set up roadblocks. Any Christmas shopping I needed to do would happen online, or not at all. Instead of sweating under fluorescent lights in Macy's and rummaging through scarves to maudlin sectarian carols, I stayed put, entombed, listened to water gurgling in the radiators and the UPS trucks grinding up the hill. I placed Nutcrackers and Santas around the house, setting up frosty scenes with candles, skaters, and reindeer, mini cathedrals and houses with little interior lights, a tiny orchestra of angels my mom had put in my stocking years ago. I sat on the kitchen floor cutting fronds of balsam and white pine and instructing my daughter how to secure them on a wire frame. I'm not the least bit handy, but I'd learned the craft as a kid and would no sooner buy a wreath than sell my dog. The Vienna choirboys' silver sound wafted through the house until abruptly replaced by Bing Crosby's blaring "White Christmas," marking an ongoing spousal rivalry, and all I could think was I knew which side Chaddy would've been on. There I sat at the kitchen table as she had done in the past five years or so when she finally accepted the benefits of letting younger hands do the work. I was in no way ready for that. But I heard her laugh, heard her say, you see? Heard her voice inside mine like blood inside a capillary wall when I told my daughter how to pour off the fat to make gravy, where the red candles were, how to time the roast.

Years earlier, on a Christmas night just twelve days after my father died, Chaddy stormed out of the house and paced the icy hills, past icicle lights trickling from colonials and Tudors and dreamy blue ones encircling plump pines, plunging her hands in her pockets, probably wishing for a cigarette as she dug herself into a pit of paranoia over the lack of cash my father had left her. Furthermore, my husband had asked about my father's accounts in light of a recent change in inheritance tax, and she had decided we were out to rob her. She reminded me of the trials of taking care of the husky, told me she'd hated the cabin in the Poconos my grandfather had built, and swore she'd be on the street if she didn't sell. Her venom was stunning. She peeled out of the driveway the next morning and didn't speak to me till Easter when I drove to her house bearing a lily, which might as well have been a stray cat. Months later I took her on a trip to London, just us. In a cheap B&B she snored breezily on the queen bed as I tossed on a soggy cot. Best days of my life, she remarked. Had I done enough? Maybe. She bought me a Shakespearean jacket and hat, which back in New York looked absurd.

Much later I remembered that her mother had always forced her to wear hats, sometimes "monstrous" ones when she was a little girl of three, four, eight—there isn't a picture of her without one. The mother I knew would not wear even a cap when temperatures dropped into the teens.

While the family bustled with dinner preparations Christmas night, I rummaged in the cedar closet for that jacket. It was burgundy velvet with richly embroidered pockets, which seemed seasonal. More critical, its puffy sleeves might go over my cast. My wardrobe choices were severely constricted. But somehow it had vanished. Twice I sifted through my husband's suits in cleaner bags, finding only my grandfather's weighty topcoat with a velvet collar, too slender for my son. At last, shivering in my sleeveless dress, I put on a huge Eddie Bauer fleece I'd given my mother and decided to retrieve when I bagged her clothes for charity. In the pocket was a treat for her terrier, who (as promised) had come to live with me. In my mind I saw her circling the pond behind the retirement community with iron determination after a hip operation, wearing that fleece and walking that dog.

The day before Christmas I went off the pain meds so I could drink wine. You'll be depressed with the withdrawal, my husband cautioned. But I wasn't—my world was off kilter anyway. This fall is self-mutilation, remarked an old friend, to distract you from emotional pain. It all makes sense. But it didn't.

My mother wouldn't let go any more than I could. I saw her as a bride during World War II, witnessed her fights with her irascible father and hot-tempered brothers, heard her guilt me on pot smoking, listened to her story of a suitor killed at war and silent implications of a different life—now, I sadly realized that her anger had its roots in pain. When she was hurt, broken, she put on a hard cast and wielded it like a weapon.

Three days after Christmas I learned the cast would come off. X-rays revealed a shortening of the wrist, and splintered pieces had moved. The whole thing would heal crooked. It wasn't the cosmetics I minded but the thought of bones and tendons not properly aligned, rubbing each other the wrong way. My new slick Manhattan surgeon recommended surgery. He'd slit my wrist, palm side, insert a plate and screws.

Ten years ago I sat in the pre-op of Bryn Mawr hospital where my mother was awaiting a hip operation. Somehow I was young enough to be struck by how vulnerable she looked in her pastel blue gown with ties dangling down the open slit in the back. I actually teared up at the sight of her doughy leg marked with a big black X. What's wrong with you? she asked edgily. I couldn't begin to say and didn't want to try. When they wheeled her away, I was sanguine once again that all would go well. I fled the hospital to walk down the village streets and stop in the old pharmacy where I used to get vanilla milkshakes in silver containers. Of course the soda fountain was long gone. My mom and I used to spin on the high red seats. She'd always buy me a treat after the dentist because I always had cavities, and no one had heard of Novocain.

I retraced my steps past Ludington Library where we used to borrow armfuls of books, slid more quarters in my meter and re-entered the too brightly lit hospital where candy-stripe volunteers welcomed me and anticipated questions I didn't need to ask. When she woke up, she smiled for an instant. You OK? Yes, she nodded, I'm fine. But you never knew.

I can't thank you enough, she said as she reached for a cup of apple juice and fumbled at the straw, her full lips so pale without her Revlon red, her words like the bread-and-butter letters she made me write to godparents after Christmas, in flawless print.

My surgery could be called routine. I arrived early in the morning (dry mouth, grumbly stomach) sat in bed watching blue interns glide by, confirmed with a dozen chart-bearing nurses that I was who I was and let them check my wristband to see if the identities matched up, and watched the scruff-jawed anesthesiologist prepare his needles. This has to be, yes, this is normal.

In a dim semi-private room unrecorded hours later, I tried to drown out my roommate's cooking shows with *Beverly Hills Housewives*. Palm Beach is such a spiritual place, cooed Kim. A nurse sped by with the gleanings of a catheter and I heard all about the proposed removal of that the next day. I stared at a brown wall covered with announcements and my name scrawled in black marker. On my thumb were the surgeon's initials. I scratched at them, didn't feel a thing. My arm was a bloated sausage bound in alarming layers of bandages—I looked like an amputee.

The block should wear off around 6, said Jimmy my nurse, who looked about thirteen. I'm here to make your meds cocktail. Oh, I've seen this before. You'll want to start the Percocet now, and then as soon as your fingers prickle—morphine shot!

At 11 p.m. with still no tingling, I swung my legs over the side of the bed and my arm dropped like a truck tire over the edge. Couldn't lift it. Couldn't move a finger. Total absence of motor skills and sensation. You could've lopped it off with a chainsaw.

I rang for Jimmy, who said I was lucky to be numb—much better than feeling. I asked for a doctor and he texted one, but she was buildings away and never arrived. Take an Ambien and forget it, advised my husband on the phone.

I couldn't forget. And numb was not better.

At 2:00, 4:00, 5:30 a.m. they took blood pressure and temperature. At 4:00 my roommate was watching someone make beef bourguignon. At 6:00 an unknown doctor told me that he hadn't heard of a block not wearing off, knock on wood, and rapped the wall. My brain fired commands: Move shoulder! Bend, fingers! My mother's voice boomed. I was inert, could do nothing. What had I lost?

By the time watery coffee and skim milk and Cheerios arrived, a faint prickling had arisen in the tips of three fingers. Warmth seeped up my arm like melting butter, like vibrato on cello strings, like the blurry gleam of a lighthouse burning through fog.

Home and off Percocet, I realized I should have kept all those baggy long-sleeve shirts of my mother's. Neither my own T-shirts nor my husband's flannel shirts would fit over the appendage I carried in a hospital sling. I tried her fleece, but it stuck. Don't, said my husband as I grabbed some scissors. You might want it again. No, never again. I slit the sleeve to the elbow. I wore it whenever I walked the terrier around the block, shuffling, soles flat on the pavement as I scanned for ice. When I told the dog to pee, I heard my voice inside hers as surely as I was wrapped in her fleece and had once been sheltered by her house and enclosed in her womb. When the splint came off I was naked, my forearm a senseless map of dead skin, my bare head exposed to January—nothing between me and the afternoon light.

Recovering Time

*T*he cold stuns my scalp and runs down my arms; blue light hits the backs of my eyelids and my arms stretch toward the basin of white ash two thousand feet beneath me—I'm inside blue. I'm inside a chip of stained glass speared by sunlight, my eyes wide open, my thighs pumping heart pumping, body like sperm charged by possibility unable to fathom distance, two thousand feet down, two thousand feet of lifeless water containing nothing but light and me, an illicit trespasser, an impulse shot through the interior of mind, a wriggling instant in a globe of time, this blueness born eight thousand years ago when Mount Mazama hurled fifty cubic kilometers of magma from her belly and created a liquid sapphire sealed within sheer mountain walls. Bubbles of light explode from my mouth and burst on the surface against sky that lights the icy water, my lungs getting tight, my feet trying to know the impossibility of touching down and the thrill of the impossibility.*

Guided boat tours cut the surface of Crater Lake. Tourists snap photos from lookout points on the scenic drive around the rim. Swimming here has always been forbidden. But in 1969, there was no one to stop us. As my brother and I scrambled down the rocks, I insisted with sixteen-year-old sagacity, "Seeing it is one level of experience; being *in* it is another." In our shorts and T-shirts we leapt from the rim of the crater, seized air in our lungs, stopped time for an instant, and plunged down until the water held.

Sometime near dawn yesterday I woke up still in the arms of a dream and tried to go back, tried to replay it before it slipped away like a fish brushing past. Turquoise saturated the backs of my eyes and seeped through my limbs. Sunlight ricocheted off water, connecting water and sky. My arms wove through currents of light and a body arched back till a face passed through open legs and emerged on the other side the way time folds around parallel events.

155

* * *

When my kids were little, bedtime was a ritual that included long baths till their fingers puckered like figs, followed by three carefully selected stories. Although they would never object to another reading of *Babar*, what they loved best was a new installment of Itchy Brother and Biggy Rat, two wily characters who ranged over the countryside getting into mischief and escaping the consequences through ingenuity and luck. Brian improvised these tales, disguising and reinventing the corporate intrigues he witnessed on his daily journeys to midtown Manhattan. The kids hooted and squirmed in their beds and begged for more, replaying them in the dark as his footsteps descended the stairs.

Tales of Brian's own childhood never assumed such vitality. When Paul and Sophie were teenagers, their eyes would meet at the dinner table with a look of weary indulgence: "Yeah, Dad, we *know* you worked on a fishing boat seven days a week when you were our age. We *know* you only got hand-me-downs from your cousins." And the unspoken subtext: we don't really care, this has nothing to do with our lives. Perhaps these anecdotes were too transparent, the message too blatant. Parents lose credibility as they are demystified.

More potent are the stories that blur the image of parent as lawmaker and arbiter of right and wrong, the stories that transport the parent out of the house and into a realm beyond their control. In my family, these stories were carefully guarded for reasons I didn't know, and to hear them we had to tiptoe out of the parlor, beyond the quotidian, and into a shadowy space that momentarily allowed such revelation. Only once or twice did my father tell me his war story, the sinking of the *Wasp* in 1942 near Guadalcanal, when he leapt from the deck of the torpedoed aircraft carrier. He never elaborated, simply told us the facts and left the rest to us, so the story became a legend, especially since we knew so little about the rest of his life. At family dinners he talked politics instead, denouncing Communism and the Soviet invasion of Czechoslovakia—which, as an antiwar, antiestablishment protestor, I heard about routinely.

In 1971 I went to Washington to protest the Vietnam War, and years later my teenage daughter often asked me about it. I told her about our conviction, the impetus to act; I tried to describe the crowds, the police on horseback, the tumult, shouts, pleas, hope, and anger. I recalled the visors of the police and their batons, the feel of my bell bottoms and Indian belt hanging off my hips as I ran to escape swirls of smoke—and that's the part she'll remember. Her mother being teargassed jostled her sense of me, as Mom.

When Sophie heard about a march at the UN to protest the pending Iraqi war, she new whom to ask and quickly persuaded me to go. Maybe it was Bush's smug assurances in 2003, his macho jingoism that recalled Nixon's vows to bomb the hell out of the Vietcong. Maybe it was simple recognition of her idealism. Early the next morning, despite single-digit temperatures, we were on a train from the suburbs to the city with families bundled in Eddie Bauer down and eight-year-olds wielding anti-war posters like social studies projects. The conductor, whose white beard bristled over the collar of his uniform, smiled and said, "This is worse than New Year's Eve."

That set the tone for the day: benign, tolerant, inclusive. We emerged from the train to find Grand Central more crowded than usual for a Saturday, and clusters of protestors chatting amicably while police waited on the sidelines and watched us file past. We walked east along 42nd Street until we hit Third Avenue and then tried to go north. Already the street was clogged with an eclectic crowd, from young couples with strollers to old guys with receding hairlines and pony-tails, guys who'd done this thirty years ago and seemed to have spent those thirty years waiting for another chance. A protestor in a stylish blue overcoat and bowler carried a poster: "Governments takes care of corporations, corporations takes care of governments, that's why war." Other signs read "No More Bushit," "Fuck Bush," "Who's the REAL terrorist?" At 50th and Third the bodies congealed into an immovable mass, and we looked wistfully east where we knew Pete Seeger was speaking, Pete Seeger who resurrected the spirit of another protest, who reminded me of friends who were drafted, others who feigned illness or insanity so they wouldn't have to kill or be killed. A group of police stood by a barrier across 50th Street. Sophie asked if the police were against the war, and I told her it was hard to say. The lines were not so clearly drawn as they'd been in Washington. The city was spending $500 million in overtime for all those cops to shepherd families around midtown. The scene was pleasant—unlikely to stop a war.

Then drums began to roll, and people began to chant.

"Whose streets?"

"Our streets!"

"Whose streets?"

"Our streets!"

Sophie's eyes lit up when a group of teenage boys clambered onto a FedEx truck that was wedged in the crowd. One ripped off his shirt and jumped up and down while lambasting Bush. A green banner advising "Make love, not war" floated past, and for a moment I basked in the cozy old optimism even as I winced at our failures and forgetfulness and impossible naiveté and words that were nothing if not satirical.

When our feet were numb, we decided to head home. But as we sat on the train and blew on our fingers, we could still feel the energy of the crowd around us, and Sophie was elated.

"Something to tell your grandchildren about," I said, and she grinned.

What I didn't say was that it would show Hussein the country wasn't behind the war. The futility of this protest was undeniable. Bush was going in. Was I deluding Sophie? Should I reiterate the lessons of Watergate and Enron, tell her that politicians lie, that we're pawns at best, that we shouldn't bother going out of our way? The rational answer was yes. The overpowering one, coming from memories of real anger and fear, was no.

In her pink terrycloth bathrobe, Sophie eagerly read the paper the next morning. "Listen, Mom," she called from the kitchen. "Police say there were 100,000 there yesterday, but the organizers say 400,000. It's always like that, right?"

* * *

That winter of 2003 the Stones were in town, and Brian and I finally decided to see them, seriously doubting how much longer they could play. Hundreds merged on the doors of Madison Square Garden as the wind bit their cheeks and heat flushed through the doorway. Once inside they loosened their scarves and hung around drinking beer from plastic cups. The crowd was predictable—balding men from Larchmont with black turtlenecks and cowboy boots, hair-teased moms in scoop-necked T-shirts and jeans, young preppies in oxford shirts and baggy khakis, dazed twelve-year-olds with parents who must have thought the kids should have the $200 experience, even though the kids didn't seem to care.

Miles from the stage, Brian and I took our seats next to a lumpy guy in a rumpled jacket who stared into space as if waiting for a plane. Spotlights flashed around the stage, a few tech guys fiddled with wiring, pop music blurred the air. Was there anything that reeked Stones? Anything that signaled the advent of those classic songs? I felt like we could have been at a Knicks game.

Finally the techies cut the lights and lit the stage, and out from behind the speakers came Jagger in a red-sequined jacket. Yes, he could still move, arms streaking overhead, feet skipping blithely over the stage, hips swiveling. He played to the ringside fans and to those in high receding tiers who clapped and screamed while leathery Keith Richards knelt over his guitar, his black shirt open to reveal his concave, drug-racked torso. Jagger pulled out "Angie," "Jumpin' Jack Flash," and "Sympathy for the Devil," and whenever the music flagged for an instant he did a sort of leprechaun hop, raising his knees, and scampering across the stage, more trickster figure than emblem of evil. Maybe half the crowd here remembered the Hells Angels at Altamont, or maybe they saw themselves driving through the night years ago, drunk out of their minds, screaming "Satisfaction"; maybe they remembered rushing to the local record store to pay $2.98 for *Sticky Fingers* and slow dancing to "Wild Horses" in someone's basement—sweaty, young, and unsure.

159

And for the other half? Jagger was a decent rock musician, maybe, a biological wonder, a sixty-year-old mopping his brow with a white towel, an icon yanked out of time and place like the Elgin Marbles, truncated horses with flexed necks, stuck on a pedestal in the British Museum.

After the secretaries screamed and the lawyers got their money's worth, after Jagger chugged some water and Charlie Watts took a dignified bow, we descended to the street where the New York night was just waking up. Clubgoers bustled in long lines waiting for doors to open. Smells of hotdogs and cigarettes and chestnuts, an ambulance siren, teens in stilettos. I dug my hands into my pockets and hustled to the car, saving traces of songs and welcoming the sail up the West Side Highway along the Hudson.

We pulled up the steep driveway as the garage door rose. Upstairs we found Sophie splayed on the couch, mesmerized by hip-hop videos on BET. To her irritation, Brian stole the remote and flicked past a few channels. Jagger appears on replay, his notorious mouth gaping across the screen as he belts out what seems a parody of "Satisfaction," his face deeply creased beneath the shock of brown hair. Too close, too staged, too slick. Had we been there? A pan of the crowd shows them clapping and rocking in place.

Sophia glanced up. "Yeah, Dad, cool."

As I left the room, I remembered sitting on Annie's bed in high school, her comforter tumbled on the floor along with frayed jeans, a dog-eared copy of *Light in August*, and the weighty *National Experience*, largely unread. She circled her knees in her toothpick arms, her silver watch and bangles that she wore, almost superstitiously, clinking on her wrist. She was torn between her boyfriend turned Buddhist and her college motorcycle man.

"Time, time, time, is on my side," pulsed the Stones, while we talked urgently, and the black disk turned round and round.

In those days you were either a Stones fan, or Beatles, or Beach Boys, and it wasn't hard to tell. Annie was Stones, no question. Since third grade, she had often slept at our house to escape the DT's and barbiturates and hurled old fashions at hers. A big green Cadillac convertible sat in the driveway and horses meandered in the paddock, but she was edgy, likely to shift moods and plans, drop acid, disappear. I remembered the day I finally accused her of taking me for granted. I was perched on the edge of my mother's bed, my fingers twisting the tangled phone cord. Annie protested and denied. I could see her thin lips and skittery blue eyes behind wire-rim glasses, her hand on her broad bony hip. I was sure she didn't even hear me. The next day her watch was gone, and beneath the bangles were thick white bandages.

Yes, time was on our side. But we couldn't see it.

Now time has taken my father, leaving me boxes of black and white photos of parts of his life I will never know. It has taken my son to college as deftly as a magician who distracts you with staging and banter while the real trick happens in a flash.

I don't miss Paul every day; I don't picture him walking through the door with his backpack, Hey Mom, as the school bus stuttered up the hill and Sophie in pink tutu raced to greet him, more blitzkrieg than ballerina. I don't think about reading his face to see what happened at school, who didn't ask him to play kickball, how the report on Poseidon went. But back when my life consisted of little but the stuff of their lives, I thought I would.

Now I walk into his room to get a sweater from the closet, thinking of nothing more sublime than doing the laundry, when I glance at his bureau and see a half-eaten pack of gum. As if he'd *just* taken a piece. Then I see his stubby fingers, the nails ripped down low, his right cheek flushed like a map of New Zealand, the paper tumbling out of his hand. I smell the musty odor when I opened the door to wake him and found him on his back like a king, a bare foot sticking out of the never-made bed. Without the 170-pound body, without his painted canvases of city streets and apparitions filtering into the night, without the stained drop cloth and heaps of clothes, the room is cavernous and sends me shuddering into the light of the hallway as surely as I first issued him into the light.

Like Paul, I have little say in the matter. Life demands living. Time boomerangs, clips you in the back of the head or lands in your fist, as one experience awakens another.

After the protest and the blizzard of 2003, it's Tuesday. Paul has been home for the weekend and not home. He spent two nights in the city with the college friend he sees every day. He's going to be home for dinner, so I buy shrimp for the dish he used to like on his birthday, Greek shrimp. But he missed his ride and has to take a train back to Providence, so we have to eat early and I have to hurry and peel the tomatoes while doing the laundry he didn't want to hassle with at college. I remember my brother's huge laundry bag spilling button-down shirts across the speckled linoleum floor when he came home from boarding school. Everyone's upstairs watching *The Simpsons*. Standing at the kitchen counter, I listen to REM sing, "The photograph on the dashboard, taken years ago, turned around backwards so the windshield shows, every streetlight reveals a picture and a verse..." I pull off the brittle skin of an onion and wait for the pasta water to boil.

At dinner we ask Paul about his friends. He glows; I've never seen him happier. Out from the yellow room that was his refuge during high school, from the press of SATs and punctilious teachers, he talks about film courses and art history and programs abroad. He mentions Jess and Caroline, Elias and Jake, and I can see the stories unfolding before his eyes while we stare eagerly and ineffectually, trying to hurry our eyes to grow accustomed to the dark so we might decipher a faint outline of his life.

Time to go, to quickly get the clothes, still damp, out of the dryer. He groans and loads them into an unfamiliar gray duffel. We shove it in the back of the car, along with his backpack and overcoat, an old cashmere one that belonged to Brian's great-uncle. We hum along 287, nearly alone on the road, most people too terrorized by the snow to venture out. I usually go 80 with music blaring. Tonight it's all slower. I see the red clock on the dashboard, don't have to hurry, the train is late, savor the time with him, the slushy sound under the wheels, the silence where the wind was two days before.

Paul says, "Do you think I could rent an apartment in the city with some friends this summer?"

"Well, better get the job first."

"Yeah, I know. But do you think you and Dad would be willing to help out?"

"Why do I want to pay more to see you less?" I say, smiling. "Anyway, your friends are all super rich."

"I know—but they want to make it on their own."

"Sounds admirable," I say, not wanting to disillusion him or malign his friends whom I don't even know. "But when the time comes, and rents are what they are, you never know."

It strikes me how they'd talked about all these things among themselves, and how much I was missing, how on frigid January nights in a cinderblock college dorm he was conceiving a life in bits and snatches. He wanted to open a restaurant, wanted to paint. Now *he* was improvising the nighttime stories.

"I might come home again before spring break," he remarks as we sit in the parking lot of the Stamford Station. But I doubt it; I think he just feels mildly guilty for spending all weekend in the city. "And thanks for dinner, it was great."

I smile, we hug, he slides out the oversized duffel. "Travel light next time," I suggest, realizing he has more there than I took to Europe for a summer of wandering at his age.

"Yeah." He smiles that irresistible smile, those brown eyes like mine. "Talk to you soon."

For a moment there is harmony and ease. We're talking. He's there. I even think about the stuff I have to do later.

But as I pull out of the parking lot, I look over and see an earnest young man trudging toward the station lights, only his head and shoulders visible above the line of taxis whose motors purr with anticipation, whose filmy exhaust swirls around his face as he passes the silhouettes of restless drivers and makes his way around piles of snow in his sneakers. And after I pull out of the parking lot, hit the first stoplight, and turn left onto 95 south to retrace my path, I rewind the movie, I see that young man carrying his duffel, catching the streetlight for an instant. And the heartbreaking thing is, it could be anyone, just someone getting on a train. Who knows that young man? Who knows what heavy dreams he lugs in that duffel? The speedometer slides past 70, I turn up the radio, it's Lennon singing: "No hell below us, above us only sky; imagine all the people living life in peace . . ."

I remember speeding north on 95 on my way to college, all by myself, a freshman, free at last. I try to remember what I thought, but I can only imagine it based on who I think I was then and what must have meant something to me. Annie gone to Wisconsin for college. We'd write, we promised. Annie in her yellow Mustang, her father hospitalized, brother overdosed, double dates one summer and the lies we told for kicks. Parties in the basement, bear hug to "Heart of Stone," driving cross country and hot air sweeping through open windows with the smell of sagebrush and sun soaked wheat.

If I don't imagine, then even the frame on which I paint these images is gone. But if I do, I'm lost in the maw of Charybdis, listening to the gulp and hiss of memory, scraping rock for an instant, being a sentiment shot through my own mind, reaching down for a springboard to return even as I know the impossibility of touching down and the ache of that impossibility.

With Her and Without

How do you throw your mother away? That's what I did yesterday. Sheer dust.

My brother and I stood by the ocean on the south shore of Long Island on a bright January morning with waves breaking hundreds of yards out, shooting spray at the sky with impetuous abandon, cresting again and pounding down on the sand like fists with splaying hands of foam that carried her away. A wave here, another there, one with her, one without. Hissing and soughing and slipping back into a tumble of brine and seaweed and deeper, maybe miles deeper, under the horizon that never flinched and maddening blue.

My mother loved the ocean. She would sit on the beach in a floral bathing suit with a skirt, elbows around her knees staring out at the waves and silently letting go. She would tuck her curls inside a bathing cap and wade into the surf, letting the waves buoy her up high above the beach, and us, jumping broken waves knee high at the edge, waiting for her to come out.

When I picked up the cardboard box that had been waiting on a shelf in the front hall closet, I was surprised by the weight. Maybe Auer Cremation supplied a hefty urn, which was included in the price. I tucked the box in the netting on the side of my trunk and drove two hours to the beach, one she never lived to see, but similar enough to the ones she had. I believed it mattered—though she had wanted no service and could not bring herself to believe in the immortality of the soul or any chance of seeing the decades cycle by with her grandchildren becoming lawyers and singers and parents and her own daughter graying and muttering nonsense and herself dying... no, it was only a hunch that the gesture or the presence of her family or the ocean itself mattered. I made the decision and felt its essential rightness but who was I to decide? And what difference does rightness make when you throw your mother away?

The cardboard packaging was wrapped so tight I needed a meat knife to cut it from one side to the other and halfway along the longer side before I could slowly pull another cardboard box from within. No metal urn, just cardboard, and inside that, a thick plastic bag with its edges sealed. A business envelope slid out containing confirmation of decease and a nameless dog tag with a number: 7649. I cut the plastic and returned the gray bag, solid as a brick, to the box until we arrived at the beach. Ten of us. Standing in a circle like Stonehenge stones, we spoke about her and remembered. I had decided to numb myself to my own words and think about tennis instead—anything but her life—but I failed with the first halting sentence. And all the while my terrier, her terrier, rolled in the sand and danced in circles and suddenly took off for the parking lot with spirited independence more typical of my mother than of her.

After the words, my brother and I walked down to the edge of the water, and the others watched. We pulled out the plastic bag. I had not cut the right seam and it was still sealed. I gouged a hole with my nail and tore. The bag was so heavy. Why did a few pounds in a 6" x 10" brick seem big?

My brother held the bag at its base with two hands and flung his arms forward sending ashes through the opening, then handed the bag to me and I did the same, back and forth we traded with ashes flying over the waves, lips of froth carrying them away, some spinning up into the wind like swirls of prairie dust until the near end when I inverted the bag and the wind that had been running across the beach shifted and flung flecks tinier than deer ticks onto my parka, which clung there, turning my evergreen jacket filmy gray. It seemed rude to brush them away.

I remembered collecting shells with my brother at the Jersey shore—the back porch reeked of dying welks, which we emptied and polished and stored in wood boxes for years until they too disappeared. I remembered wanting to take my mother from the nursing home back to the shore for a day and never making the two hour drive plus two more and back again because it was easier not to—I pictured her smiling and squinting at the ocean and breathing the wind from all across the Atlantic instead of the air where no one opened a window. I tried to shake the image the way a dog shakes off rain but there she was. There she was gazing at her life as if it were the ocean she had crossed in a ship at age three to begin a life here. I remembered her impetuous spirit, which was as obvious and constant to her as waves rolling onto a shore whether I stood there or not, whether sapphires danced on the water or onxy waves heaved at the shore and fell back unseen again and again through every night of every year—and how could that, too, disperse? I picked up a fistful of sand and squeezed till the grains pricked my palm. The terrier jumped at my shins and gulls hung on the wind, their white backs catching the light, their wings outstretched as if doing nothing at all. I waited, distracted.

How do you turn around and walk up the beach and meet your children's eyes after throwing your mother away?

In the Walls

When Brian came to my family's cabin in the Poconos, and clouds moved in, and rain hit the mud roads like shotgun pellets, he'd sigh and bury himself in *The Magus*. He referred to it as a land of dripping pines and hankered for the ocean, possibly the only aspect of his roots he hadn't severed when he went off to college. Sophia was conceived by the sea and somehow *Moby-Dick* became her favorite novel with all its fastidious descriptions of rigging and knots and whale blubber, which is especially bizarre since she is (and always was) far from patient. The other half, Paul and I, love labyrinthine woods and paths and sun dappled brooks trickling under rhododendron and ferns. We're the more introverted ones, so I suppose in a Romantic paradigm, this affinity makes sense. Father and daughter, on the other hand, melt as their toes touch sand. Sophie lathers on Coppertone and dares the sun in her string bikini from J. Crew; Brian in battered fedora sets up his beach chair and looks as if the ocean just expected him to come and feels relief at the sight of him as he sighs and pops a beer. It's almost funny how quickly their souls are at rest.

How could a wife stand in the way of that?

For years Brian wanted a beach house, and for years we couldn't afford one. Then I simply didn't want one. I didn't want to pack up the wilting lettuce and jeans and dog food on a Friday night and start Sunday thinking about doing the same in reverse. I wanted to travel, not acquire, give away stuff from the existing house, not buy everything again for a second one. One can always find a reason not to do something. Finally I realized I didn't have a good enough one to deflate a dream.

We bought a shingle house, which had been rented to a professor who apparently was oblivious to everything except maritime law and his two enormous dogs, who left us a heritage of dog hair and scratched wood and half-chewed rawhide bones. I doubt anyone had painted since the house was built in the early '90s. Grease rimmed the muntins, cracks ventured up several walls and across ceilings, and whatever color the walls originally were had become flesh-toned, a sort of non-color that is hard to imagine anyone would deliberately pick, and maybe no one had.

I wanted the living room to be heaven, diaphanous gray in winter and early morning blue in summer. I streaked one wall with indigo and silver and robin's egg blue samples and shook my head as they dried. For the rest, I deferred to the family who bought magazines showing white rooms with marshmallow fluffy couches and Renovation Hardware sisal rugs on walnut-stained floors and tables made out of wood from old barns to which another generation would have set fire.

When June arrived and another flock of my students dispersed for the summer and beyond, I drove to the beach to paint. The sky that first day was like tin. No one was there. The fridge held a can of Coke and a jar of pickles. The kids were at work in Manhattan, and Brian would come out the following night. A guy who'd worked on the exterior had left a ghostly film of plaster on the sea-blue sink and an empty vodka bottle in the garage, our vodka. I tied back my hair, kicked off my flip-flops, and hit Vampire Weekend on Pandora because those songs were like skipping stones—all beat and energy and melody you could hum without a connected thought. Then Jack White sang about the playground with retro innocence, and the Blow was crooning you were out of my league, and I dreamt about that while stirring my gummy creamy paint. Simply white. That's what I started with and that was the name of the paint: Simply White. Not a white with hues of tepid pink or chilly blue, just Easter lily pure.

Between songs I heard nothing except the icemaker's sporadic ca-chunk and my bare feet on wood as I searched for a liner for the roller pan. The house was skeletal and vaguely enticing. In the corners were dust mites of other lives, unseen fingerprints on window ledges, a box of Kleenex half used under a sink, a too large dog dish and rubber bones with teeth imprints like fossils. I never knew what I'd find behind a door or in a closet that by contract had been cleaned out, but as with Bluebeard's castle, when night came on, so did a not unpleasant ill ease, as if the lunar moth fanning the window pane outside were more at home than I. It was all in limbo, that's what I liked. It felt out of time but not timeless, and I liked that too. A hollow feeling, like being just a little hungry. I walked with purpose through boxes of space as if through shadows of an underworld that I would revisit later and say, yes, I've been here before, only now I recognize where I am—just as I knew one day I'd know each limb of the white pines jutting across the driveway and tangling with the oaks overhead, know them the way you know the shape of your children's toes.

In the garage I found a high-powered adjustable light, which I positioned in the corner of Paul's room. From there its cyclopean eye gleamed on the wall, which stared back with the opacity of pancake batter and comparable indifference. Armed with Fantastik and rags and assuming a crab-like squat, I inched around the room, scrubbing the rim of the baseboard and a parallel line of dirt entrenched in the molding. With a rusty putty knife from the other house, I put a blob of spackle in a crack, nudged it in and gently wiped away the excess so that no one would know the crack ever existed and I would probably forget. Then I stirred my vanilla milkshake paint again so the density at the top felt equal to that at the bottom, and poured a hefty amount into the immaculate plastic liner. I laid the roller in the tray and gingerly advanced toward the pool of paint, barely touching its outer margins, then rolled in a bit farther till the pink fuzz was covered in white but not submerged. Back and forth the roller hissed till it assumed an even coat. And when I lifted my arm for that first definitive stroke, no drops fell to disrupt the momentary pleasure of an even thrust and the silky sighs of wet paint leaving the roller and creating a roadway down the wall. At the time the process didn't strike me as quite this sexual but maybe it was, me in my flimsy T-shirt and twilight bearing down on the windows and that single beam of light pouring itself onto the walls and Eddie Vedder filling the boxes of space with his voice as rich as pecan pie singing about being a fool and seeing his love on the other side.

Sometime later I found myself pausing with paint-splashed limbs in the middle of a bare white room. My first wall stared back at me, sedate and dry, while the last one last answered the spotlight with a gentle sheen. The scene was hardly spectacular, poor understated room affecting a facelift but left embarrassed by unpainted woodwork and used paper towels scattered about. So be it. Change takes time, I tried to believe, and I wouldn't create order for its own sake in medias res.

With that first decrescendo, painting (like grocery shopping or raising kids) took on the benign gratification of routine. I got so used to it all, I could stir and scrub and dip and roll with mind numbing consistency. Yet I wasn't numb. I watched my hand dip the brush, scrape the paint from one side, pass evenly down the side of a window frame, gauging just how much pressure to apply to splay the bristles to cover the molding without touching the wall, an estimation dependent in part on the amount of paint on the brush which is naturally an ever changing variable. And while I saw to it that not a line wiggled, not a blob traveled out of my control, my mind was somewhere shifting and swerving like an offshore wind that throws a boat off course or leaves it becalmed, nothing revelatory, just images of the old cabin in the mountains, of Paul as artist painting in his room with the door tight shut, of catching waves with my brother at the Jersey shore years ago, of the other guy who lives who knows where, and of Brian's anxious eyes as he waited to hear if we'd gotten the house.

I took pride in being a purist, which was weird given the transient nature of the job. I scoffed at painter's tape and the wedges hardware stores push for covering windowpanes, both of which urge you to whip on the paint with complete faith and high speed. Knowing that globules of paint would sneak under the tape, only to ridicule me the following day, I chose tortoise methodology over hare. With my son's tiny artist brush bearing mere molecules of paint, I plodded along the tops and bottoms and sides of each muntin on each pane, never calculating time and distance, perversely savoring the crick in my neck or announcement by a dormant calf muscle that it existed, or the tingling in a finger that lost circulation, odd ways to remember one is alive, yet comfortingly discrete compared with the cerebral twinges of my teaching life. Each dip in the woodwork screamed caution and each blip in my brushwork demanded correction, immediate correction, as if it mattered, when in any rational moment anyone would tell me otherwise, including me.

I put white semi-gloss on the woodwork in Paul's room and finished before the weekend when he brought his new girlfriend, the one he would marry, to the house. In the afternoon light of inglorious victory, I gathered paint-crusted paper towels and scraped paint flecks from the floor. My room was next. Following in my son's footsteps, I went with Simply White, which looked airy, luminous, and beach-journal worthy. Meanwhile, Sophia was asserting her identity and testing out colors in accordance, streaking her startled walls with the whim of the day, be it lemon or butter, rose or lavender, gray cloud or Nantucket sky. Her room became the coat of many colors, a kaleidoscope of personality, or indecision. Her distressed side tables and silver lamps with motorcycle studs arrived, which complicated the color choice and set us back a few days—plus the bathroom had to be coordinated with the bedroom, which would not have crossed my mind. Within the same family, some lived more immediately than others in the physical world.

The summer wore on, and sweat poured off.

A few carpenters and painters were working outside and I sometimes wondered what they thought of this middle-aged woman in her little shorts lugging paint cans and rinsing out brushes with a hose. Somehow *their* arms and shins were never coated in paint. We'd chat, wave—mostly I didn't want them to take my drop cloths. I found myself indignant watching a guy spend the whole day stroking paint onto the front door, and fiercely critical when I noted drips of paint on the deck or blears on the windowpanes outside. I scrutinized exterior molding and railings, smugly pointing out omissions to my husband, who nodded with incredulity.

At length Sophie settled on lavender, and I wondered what had happened to the understated taste with which I had raised her, but said nothing. Still, the hunt continued. Within the lavender family were iris and purple whispers and hints of heaven, names reminiscent of a romance series, and little sample jars continued to accumulate on her windowsills. Temperatures soared. My husband swam in the bay, my daughter sat at her computer in the city in a wool sweater and boots. I blasted Vampire Weekend, hauled the step ladder around the room, let the breeze from the wetlands sift through the screens and mingle with the smell of coffee, watched the light as it left one wall and slanted across another, turning the lavender pearly blue or purply gray. I became grateful for nuance, and frankly when the job was done and my daughter arrived, we walked into a room as if into a piece of the sky—as if color were fragrance rather than pigment with a power to transport.

I put my feet on the railing of the deck and drank a beer and ate some chips.

By now I knew when the sun threw squares of light across the bed like a poker hand. By now I recognized nicks in the floorboards and the creak of the back door. By now I knew how absurdly easy it was to transform mood. Here were my paint flecks on the floor and memory of cracks patched and sanded; here, too, was an old green rocker from the cabin that I had decided to leave flat forest green.

I thought of teaching and how you never knew, of writing a story and how you never knew. One student told me she learned how to read the world. Another, who didn't tell me, erased my name with the first blast of summer. Others came back years later or wrote emails from distant places that something some professor said reminded them of something I'd said, and it feels like ghosts not of them but of myself traveling in wisps here and there as randomly as my thoughts when I had rolled out roadways of paint.

One night about a year later, I was taking a bath and noted a spot where the blue-green line just under the ceiling molding quavered. This room had been my greatest challenge with the shower stall to outline and the rim around the bath and over the sink. I nearly leapt out of the water to find the paint, but the warmth flowed around and I sank lower and closed my eyes. I knew it didn't matter, and the all consuming feeling that it did belonged to the house—it was in the walls, behind sinks and inside closets, like primer under a finished coat.

As water gurgled in the drain, I dried off and thought about the potatoes to make, the dill to chop, the table to set with rainbow-striped mats that Paul had given me. I thought about setting candles on the table and going outside to find nepeta and daisies to put in a jar. I'd feel the gravel underfoot and the uneven stone walkway through the grass in the back yard, note brown needles at the base of a white pine bitten by winter ice, hear the brazen chirruping of peepers, watch the terrier get up and slowly move to the shade cast by a chair in the evening light, hear Sophia's barrel laugh and Paul's even voice on the phone, and all these things would feel not like things but colors, intangible colors whose shades I would witness as my children have children and as Brian watches the light on the water and feels at home.

Pokie

She is no longer "the terrier," the white dog that used to dash down the hallway of my mother's apartment building when she saw me coming, or the mildly curious white dog who stepped out of her bed in the nursing home when I arrived. I'd give her a few pats as she stood on her hind legs, front paws on my shins, smiling with tipped back ears and eyes that looked right into mine as few people dare—and then she'd return to her grimy green bed, curl up, and close her eyes, whether asleep or not, I didn't consider. Everyone loved her in the skilled nursing wing of the retirement home. She was the liveliest thing going in those corridors of open doors and tepid food trays and droning TVs. Sometimes a lady down the hall took her for the night, or so I was told. I didn't really think about how the terrier liked that, but now I do. Now I know she is a dog of a thousand emotions, a dog who has come to own her name and teach me a thing or two.

Pokie was born at a breeder's house somewhere on the outskirts of the Main Line. Although I don't know the sordid details, Chaddy said the pup lived in a crate in a basement for the first year of her life—why, I have no idea. So, although my mother paid for the dog, she essentially rescued her. Initially terrified of everyone and everything, the dog kept to herself, curling up in a patch of sun on the carpet and reluctantly going for walks only when my mother snapped on a leash and gave her a tug. Behind my mother's apartment was a pond the color of mint sauce and a walkway that circled it and wound up around other efficient brick buildings. Once out of sight of the residents, Chaddy would let Pokie off the leash, and the puppy, relishing but not abusing her freedom, would dash into the woods after a chipmunk or sniff around a resident's pachysandra or trot up to a sluggish wheelchair—and eventually rejoin my mother. Unlike the West Highlands we had as I grew up, this one never ran away and never yapped. You'd wonder if, in fact, she was the same breed, but her looks precluded the slightest doubt. She was a model Westie who might have posed for Hallmark with her square face, short snout, and earnest brown eyes that betrayed nothing but endearing innocence. And she was petite, a mere 14 pounds. Chaddy could easily lift her up, plop her on the passenger seat of her Toyota, and drive her around as she went to the cheese shop or stopped at Bryn Mawr College for a brisk walk. She drove her miles to have her properly groomed—plucked not clipped—being as solicitous of her puppy's appearance as she once had been of mine. For months Chaddy patted, encouraged, trained, and talked to Pokie, successfully socializing her so that no one ever would have guessed her troubled past.

Now, two years after my mother's death, I have come to know the World According to Pokie—in particular, her Thirteen Virtues (herein Eleven) enacted more consistently by this old dog than by the illustrious Founding Father who imagined the perfectibility of Man.

For the first year she lived with me, Pokie slept and slept. Finding a sunken white armchair from my mother's apartment to be a viable bed, she'd sit before it, start forward once, twice, gauging the jump like a kid cradling a basketball in anticipation of a foul shot, then launch herself onto the pillow where she'd curl up, tucking her chin under her back legs. There she hibernated, warm, snug, and solitary as a box turtle until hunger urged her to come down or I decided she should go out. My husband, who refused to acknowledge her as a legitimate canine (being undersized), did not even know she was there, little ghost that she was. She never whined or complained, never used her troubled childhood as an excuse to break the law, never envied others or relapsed into self pity. I thought she was content, just old. She had me fooled.

Some friends visited the other day with a fluffy Bijon Frise with hair like a Fragonard aristocrat in a powdered wig. This antsy little thing scurried under the table for crumbs and whined at the door when Brian lit up the grill and threw on some steaks. The dog's owner told me she—the dog—has granola, Cheerios, and milk for breakfast, prime ribs and sautéed vegetables for dinner. In the Hamptons she finds New York strip steak at a boutique market called Red Horse and makes deliberate trips for her Bijon Frise. On that day when they came to lunch, Pokie lay by a pot of pink geraniums on the deck, shifting position only when the midday sun saturated her white coat and she settled under the shade of a chair. She didn't bat an eye at the goat cheese and crackers set on a low cocktail table. On a daily basis she simply reminds me—with a little extra attention, nothing more—when it's 3:00 and time for a cup of kibble and a scoop of Mighty Dog. Often she exhibits outright excitement, dancing around my legs and dashing to the dish as I set it down. She proceeds to eat with dignity, never gulping her food, and often leaving some for a later snack. Sameness does not dampen her imagination.

Some evenings—and I can never predict when—Pokie receives her little biscuit and turns it into a mouse. She grabs the prey, dashes into the living room, drops it, picks it up again and flicks it a foot or two. She might wander away, giving the mouse a final chance, suddenly trot back and take it gingerly in her jaw. Then she lies down, biscuit between her front paws, gives it a lick, takes a bite.

In Pokie's universe, size is not a measure of courage. She approaches huskies and Bernese and feral cats with unilateral, unequivocal audacity. My neighbor keeps emailing me that I should kill these cats, born under the hose box in my back yard. For years the cats and Fin, my Portuguese Water Dog, had an unspoken understanding about acceptable space, but wild balls of fur would dart out from large hosta plants or skim past my peripheral vision on the wall outside. A black and white one staring at me head-on made me wonder if my house was my own. My neighbor sends me articles saying sterilization is the current thinking, but what would that do for these potential rabies-carrying cats that stalk my yard? Call the Humane Society, or a shelter? No sane person would adopt them. I consider my options: call, not call, tell her to call, tell her I called. Fin weighed 55 pounds and stood about three feet tall at the shoulder. I loved his tolerance, gentle spirit, and democratic love of humanity, but that sensibility didn't underlie his passivity with cats. I am fearful of killing them, and so was he. The summer he died, the cats were still in residence, and a few months later, Pokie arrived. Cat sightings are scarce now. The other day a mustard calico with a lion's mane crept along the wall of a planter in the back yard. Pokie's head rose from her nap. In an instant she leapt off the deck, charged about ten feet, and stopped stock-still. She didn't *need* to get close. If she did, it would not go well for Pokie, but for some reason the cat, who turned and slid through the rhododendron, still doesn't know.

Pokie doesn't flaunt her will, she exhibits it when she wills for explicit and largely reasonable reasons. Because she is nearly blind and deaf, her world is a network of olfactory stimuli like an air traffic controller's map of New York. When I take her for a walk, out of the familiar house and yard, she malingers, then stops abruptly. I pull, she's locked in place. I pull harder, nope. She wins. Leash slackened, she walks to the side of the road for a crucial smell and a pee whose imperative is territorial and nothing more. She safeguards her strong will, having learned from the best.

Pokie wouldn't dream of barking at a passerby or the mailman. She doesn't succumb to futile bravado. She utters a sharp, articulate message only when she wants to come in and waits mere seconds between barks. Instantly I pull myself up from the sofa. Selective demands further her cause, and she is clear in her desire. She is like a little Greek traveler who by age-old tradition expects one thing on her journey: *xenia.* Really, she shouldn't have to ask.

For years in the nursing home, Chaddy sat in a wheelchair, sleeping more than a dog. She couldn't lean down to pat Pokie. Although I reminded the dog walker to pick up the terrier and put her in my mother's lap now and then, I wasn't there to see that carried out and, according to Chaddy, it wasn't. She had no control over the daily schedule that took her out of her room, left her at lunch for several hours and sitting in a hallway before and after the meal for several more. And due to the volatile health of old people, the aides rarely took my mother out. When I visited, I'd wheel her around the grounds, pointing out systematically planted impatiens, and Pokie would come, too. If we sat outside the front door watching visitors and ambulances come and go, Pokie lay down and watched with unflinching calm. After this near-death monotony, she moved to the Elysian Fields. Summers I often take her to the beach in the evening where she rubs her head in the sand and then throws her whole body into it, rolling, wriggling, thrashing, and suddenly rights herself, staring to see if I see. Then she rolls again, shakes, and meanders off to sniff a rock. I walk on down the beach, looking back to be sure she is there. At age thirteen she goes at her own pace and can't hear me even if I call. On my way back I clap, a sound that somehow travels the ear canal and manages to awaken her inner ear. Then I squat, the signals click in her brain, and she dashes towards me, all smiles, ears back, leaping and tripping on the tire-rutted sand. She doesn't stop when she reaches me, but jumps a little, never taking her eyes off me, and keeps going, inviting me to run. Sometimes she dashes in circles around me, halting abruptly and switching directions to outwit me.

Pokie seizes these moments with pure *joie de vivre*. Yet if I changed my mind, leash in hand, and decided to have a cup of coffee, she would swiftly lie down (all four legs collapsing back in one efficient motion) as if we'd never had a plan. She's *so* zen, I'm tempted to think, equating the word with easy going, even tempered, living in the present, tranquil, all qualities I singularly lack and my mother actively disdained. Pokie lay by Chaddy's bed as she declined, slept softly on her bed at night. Pokie was there—scouting for crumbs or lifting her head at the smell of a passerby or lapping stale water—she was there when my other died; I was not.

Suffering, loneliness, and death inspired the Buddha's first Noble Truth. The Second attributes suffering to ignorance and greed. I cannot begin to say what Pokie knows or doesn't; instead, I infer levels of awareness from the facts of her existence, which is clearly inadequate and highly speculative, and deny her the ability to reason. But I've noticed she shies away from most men. At worst, her ears go back and she quietly leaves the room, creeps up the stairs, and retreats to an armchair. Some element of her past—I suspect abuse—informs that behavior, call it conditioning or knowledge or just an impulse crackling along a pathway blazed years ago. Despite ill treatment, she keeps her cool, but her gentle retreat belies more than a momentary reaction to a stranger.

I don't know what that semi-sleeping state actually is in which most dogs spend their days, but somehow, as if emerging from meditation with perceptions washed clean, Pokie, motionless, eyes closed, intuits when I leave the room. She knows. She senses absence, palpably. Sometimes she isn't sure where I've gone, and as I hustle from room to room cleaning or grabbing a sandwich, I might find her standing adrift, staring into space like my mother. Other times, she detects the trail and surprises me. I open the bathroom door and there she is— lying down, front paws stretched in front, head resting but eyes alert, waiting. Maybe she reasons that I, too, could disappear. But just as the Third Noble Truth relies on confidence in the Buddha's teaching, Pokie trusts I will appear, and rises to greet and follow me when I do.

Pokie is the survivor, the last of a generation. My mother and all the other Westies have died, as have my mother's brothers—Dick who left us his golden lab when he went off to live in Caracas—and Chad who had dachshunds and retired to Vermont. Long dead is my mother's mother, the initiator of the terrier tradition with her line of handsome Scotties. Now Pokie is the matriarch, the bearer of lives lost, dignified and self possessed. When I open the door in the morning, she stands at the threshold, gauging temperatures and the day's stimuli of deer and drying hydrangea and car exhaust borne in by a breeze or sudden gust. I wait. She waits. Come on, I urge, and she steps gingerly over the doorway and onto the deck. At the steps, she stares down, as if estimating the distance for the first time. She starts forward, hesitates, then hops down three stairs in even succession. She waddles across the driveway as idly as her name suggests, does her business and kicks up gravel with her hind legs. Her good manners are instinctual if not always accurate. She takes her time.

I awoke in the middle of the night recently to hear her faintly yipping in her sleep. What do dogs dream? Does she hear in her dreams though not in waking life? Does she greet the big black dog she saw today, or is her subconscious all fluid and amorphous sensation? Does she ever return in her dreams to those years with my mother, circling the pond, or trailing after the dog walker as my mother dozed? Some people put dogs down when the owner dies, believing the dog will be crushed. Pokie defies expectation with poise. This little inconsequential dog has shown me that the key word is not *transcend* (the Fourth Noble Truth), but *embrace:* to not only live in the present, in the orange light of a moon eclipsed, or halt at a precipice in the past, paralyzed by memory, or prepare for a future that reaches a bluff and curls out of my line of vision, but to keep looking, looking, often with no map and no sense of direction. When Pokie is ambling down the beach, unsure who the figure is by the water, I kneel on the pebbles and cracked clams and welks and stretch my arms as wide as I can.

Acknowledgments

I extend wholehearted thanks to my editor and publisher, Edward Myers, for his enthusiasm and unflagging support, scrupulous attention to detail, and commitment to the survival of the essay as a legitimate genre. With characteristic generosity, Christine Matthäi provided the cover photograph for the book, and I thank her warmly both for her inspired work and frequent advice to follow one's passion. My gratitude goes to Ann Hyman and Charlotte Mayerson for their faithful reading and feedback over the years; to Alina Shevlak for her astute editorial comments; and to Vadim Serebro for the inspiration to write again, persistent faith in me, and candor when I failed. I am deeply indebted to my children, Paul and Sophia, who supported and celebrated this endeavor, and to my husband, Brian, whose patience with my syntactical battles, keen editorial eye, calm reassurance on a daily basis, and advice on every step of the publishing process were invaluable.

About the Author . . .

Caroline Sutton's essays have appeared in *North American Review, Cimarron Review, The Pinch, The Literary Review, Ascent, Southwest Review,* and *Tampa Review*. "Eclipsed," included here, received *Southern Humanities Review*'s Theodore Christian Hoepfner Award. Formerly an editor at Charles Scribner's Sons, Sutton teaches creative nonfiction at The Masters School and lives in Dobbs Ferry, New York.

About Montemayor Press

Montemayor Press is an independent publisher of literature for children and adults. To learn more about our books, visit

www.MontemayorPress.com

or write for a catalogue at:

Montemayor Press
P. O. Box 546
Montpelier, VT 05601

www.ingramcontent.com/pod-product-compliance
Lightning Source LLC
Chambersburg PA
CBHW021054090426
42738CB00006B/337